SECRET SOLDIERS

How the U.S. Twenty-Third Special Troops Fooled the Nazis

PAUL B. JANECZKO

CANDLEWICK PRESS

First edition 2019

Library of Congress Catalog Card Number 2018961335
ISBN 978-0-7636-8153-1

19 20 21 22 23 24 LSC 10 9 8 7 6 5 4 3 2 1

Printed in Crawfordsville, IN, USA

This book was typeset in Lucida.

Candlewick Press
99 Dover Street
Somerville, Massachusetts 02144

visit us at www.candlewick.com

For Lynn Plourde,
dear friend, wordsmith, guide,
and a member in good standing
of the A-1 Diner Writing Group

In memoriam
Kim Mathews (1951–2017)

CONTENTS

INTRODUCTION

1944: The large army truck stopped at the swing gate, its engine idling in the frigid February night while its headlights lit up a sign:

STOP
NO ADMITTANCE
WITHOUT WRITTEN AUTHORITY
OF COMMANDING OFFICER
ARMY EXPERIMENTAL STATION

The men sitting in the back of the truck had little idea why they'd been brought to Pine Camp, a huge army base in northern New York State, about fifteen miles from the Canadian border. The men knew that they had been chosen for this assignment because of the high scores they had achieved on the mechanical and mental aptitude tests when they were accepted into the Army Specialized Training Program (ASTP). The soldiers had been personally interviewed and selected by Colonel Hilton Howell Railey, the commanding officer (CO) of Pine Camp and, by many accounts, "the most popular and interesting of the officers" in the program. The swing gate lifted as the driver jammed the transmission into first gear and the truck lurched into the Army Experimental Station.

One of the men who had arrived at Pine Camp was Lieutenant Richard Syracuse, a "tall, muscular man with a flamboyant manner" who was commissioned as an officer at age twenty. Like the others in the truck, he had no idea why they had been recruited and brought to this out-of-the-way base. As an officer, he wanted to know what his assignment would be at Pine Camp.

Syracuse reported to Colonel Railey's office. But before he could get an explanation from his CO, Railey told the young lieutenant to follow him.

The two drove to an observation point on a remote hill, where they waited in the quiet darkness. Then out of the night came the distant rumbling of a powerful diesel engine. A tank! Then another. More tank engines snarled to life in the darkness, the vehicles apparently crawling up the hill toward their position. Syracuse stared into the distance, following the growing roar of dozens of tanks. Did he *see* the tanks? Did he see "shadowy forms . . . emerging from the tree line"? Many years later, Syracuse still remembered what happened next. "Suddenly my ears are telling my eyes that there are tanks out there," he recalled. "Is it possible for your ears to tell your eyes to see something?"

But there were no tanks rumbling up that hill in the snowy night. And *that,* Syracuse found out, was what the AES was all about. Creating sonic deceptions. Using the sounds of war machines and equipment and troops as part of a deception operation that would fool the German army into believing what their ears told them.

The sonic unit training at the Army Experimental Station at Pine Camp, New York, was but one of four units of the Twenty-Third Headquarters Special Troops. The other units were a camouflage battalion, a signal operations company, and a combat engineer company, all of which were being trained at Camp Forrest, Tennessee. The Twenty-Third included actors, painters, set designers, camouflage experts called *camoufleurs,* and assorted tricksters. Their ultimate mission was to move into an area, secretly take the place of a fighting unit, and then—with their bag of tricks, including inflatable tanks, pyrotechnics, camouflage, spoof radio plays, special effects, and sonic deception—pretend they were the unit they had replaced.

In the meantime, the fighting unit would circle around the German troops and attack them from behind or at their flank. In the words of one of its officers, Fred Fox, the Twenty-Third was "more theatrical than military . . . like a traveling road show," which would, over the course of the war, perform more than twenty times in the European Theater of Operations (ETO), impersonating real fighting units.

But how, as World War II loomed, did the United States decide that it needed such a deception unit? The U.S. military had long held, after all, that deception in war was underhanded, somehow un-American. How did the army find the men with the artistic talents to be part of the camouflage unit of the Twenty-Third? Where did they find the men with sonic expertise to reproduce the sounds of battle? Who were the communications troops who would create and broadcast fake messages? And who were the commanding officers who got the four units of the Twenty-Third to function as a team on the battlefields of Europe? The answers to these questions tell the tale of the Twenty-Third Headquarters Special Troops.

This band of U.S. soldiers, who came to be known as the Ghost Army, played a dangerous game of fooling the Nazi army into making battlefield mistakes that would eventually cost Germany the war. The story of these heroic men remained a government secret for more than fifty years.

CHAPTER 1

THE GHOST ARMY IS BORN

On September 1, 1939, German troops poured into Poland like an angry sea, and World War II in Europe began. By the end of the year, Adolf Hitler's forces had occupied Hungary and Czechoslovakia as well. Then, after a relatively quiet winter, the war roared back to life in the spring of 1940 as the German army swept through Denmark, Norway, Belgium, Holland, Luxembourg, Yugoslavia, Greece, and France. With Hitler's new conquests, only fifty miles of the English Channel stood between his troops and England. To help make up for what they lacked in soldiers and equipment, the British turned to deception.

The U.S. military establishment, on the other hand, felt a disdain for deception, believing that it somehow ran contrary to the American character, which insisted on "fair play," even in war. However, a handful of U.S. generals were beginning to reconsider the usefulness of deception in battle.

Some historians say that the U.S. military began to rethink its position after the decisive British defeat of German field marshal Edwin Rommel, known as the "Desert Fox," in North Africa in October 1942—a defeat largely made possible by a set of British deception efforts called Operation BERTRAM (September–October 1942).

When the United States entered the war in Europe in December 1941, it declined to coordinate the Allied deception operations through the London Controlling Section (LCS) of MI5, the British Security Service, and formed its own group to control its deception ops: the Joint Security Committee, later renamed the Joint Security Control (JSC). The JSC included top officers from the U.S. Army, Air Force, and Navy. Each selected a high-ranking officer as an assistant.

As its name suggests, the main goal of the Joint Security Control was protecting the security of military information, to keep it from falling into enemy hands. In addition, the JSC was to coordinate cover and deception operations of the military and nonmilitary agencies in the United States. With the JSC established, the stage was set for the creation of the Twenty-Third Headquarters Special Troops.

Major Ralph Ingersoll, who worked in London in the operations branch of the army's headquarters, wasn't shy about taking credit for originating the concept for a "super secret battalion of specialists in the art of manipulating our antagonists' decisions." Ingersoll referred to this unit as "my con artists." But was Ingersoll really responsible for creating the deception unit that came to be the Twenty-Third Headquarters Special Troops?

Since Ingersoll had a "reputation for exaggerating his accomplishments," Rick Beyer, a Ghost Army authority, believes that Ingersoll "certainly didn't conceive of the Ghost Army all on his own." He worked with Colonel William "Billy" Harris, at the orders of General Jake Devers, commander of the headquarters of the American army in Europe (ETOUSA), who insisted that the time was right to appoint a permanent cover and deception officer for the European Theater of Operations.

Major Ralph Ingersoll

Harris's first task was to assess the role that deception should play in the ETO. Harris issued a report that recommended formation of a deception unit "capable of simulating one corps [about fifty thousand men], consisting of one infantry division and one armored division, by means of prefabricated portable dummies together with the appropriate radio communications." In the end, it was Devers who endorsed the idea and sent his approval in a memo to the War Department on December 24, 1943. Military historian Jonathan Gawne notes, "Lots of people suggest things, but it was Devers that had his name at the bottom of the memo" that went to Washington. Despite the endorsement from Devers, it was still nearly two years before the U.S. deception unit was fully operational. The U.S. military simply did not have the manpower it needed at that point to quickly move the operation forward.

Oddly enough, it was the work of two others—neither a career military man but each with strong social connections with people in high places in Washington, D.C.—that laid the foundation for what was to become the Ghost Army.

Douglas Fairbanks Jr. was a man of action. The dashing and popular movie star was known for his portrayal of intrepid and swashbuckling heroes who were always at the ready to protect merchant ships from marauding pirates. So with a second world war looming, Fairbanks wanted to be part of it. His interest in joining the armed forces was no gimmick to boost ticket sales of his movies. He wanted to serve his country.

Fairbanks explained in *The Salad Days,* an autobiography covering his early life and his activities in World War II, that he had actually wanted to join the navy before the war started. "All my life," he wrote, "I had loved the lure of the sea . . . and almost everything to do with ships." He rejected service in the other branches for practical reasons. The Army Air Corps wasn't a good fit for him because he admitted that he knew "next to nothing about flying and wasn't particularly anxious to learn." Thanks to his family's connections in Washington, he could have taken "some relatively easy-to-get commissions in the Army," but Fairbanks knew that the army required lots of marching, and he hated to walk!

Having chosen the navy, Fairbanks set his sights on commissioning as an officer. However, because he didn't have the formal education that the navy required of its officers, that door was closed to him. But a family friend did let him in on a secret: men interested in becoming naval intelligence officers didn't need that education. The movie star enlisted immediately and was commissioned on April 10, 1941, as a lieutenant junior grade in the U.S. Naval Reserve.

Once in the navy, Fairbanks let it be known that he wished to be "of service in any capacity." His family's political connections came in handy again when Undersecretary of State Sumner Welles reported Fairbanks's intense interest in serving President Roosevelt, a friend of Fairbanks's parents. Welles believed that Fairbanks might be an ideal person for the State Department to send on what could be billed as a fact-finding trip to a number of South American countries. According to Fairbanks, the "official line" was that he could go to South America to "further develop cultural relations" on behalf of the United States and "meet and exchange views with painters, sculptors, writers, theater and film people."

However, since, as Fairbanks was informed, "nearly two million people in South America . . . had recently come from Germany," the real reason for his trip was more clandestine. He was to find out, "in whatever offhand manner" he could, whether the countries he visited would be sympathetic to the United States if the country were attacked or became actively involved in the war. And "most important," he recalled, "I was to find out if we would be welcome in that country if we needed to use its ports as possible emergency repair bases for our navy."

Fairbanks visited Brazil, Argentina, Uruguay, Chile, and Peru during his trip that lasted ten weeks, from mid-April to the end of June 1941. Back in the United States, he filed a report to Welles, who shared it with the president. According to Fairbanks, he received "nothing but praise" from the administration for his clandestine work. "I was very pleased indeed," he recalled, "and wondered, 'What next?'" The answer was not long in coming.

>>>

GERMANS IN SOUTH AMERICA

It might seem odd that the U.S. Navy would send Lieutenant Douglas Fairbanks Jr. to South America in 1941 to gather intelligence. After all, the United States wasn't even in the war and neither were any of the countries on that continent. However, U.S. foreign policy and military leaders decided they needed to keep tabs on countries that had ties to Hitler's Germany, in particular Argentina.

Since the late 1800s, Argentina had been a "favored land" for German emigration. The demise of many German institutions following the country's loss in World War I made emigrating attractive to many Germans. The "long, bloody and wearisome" war had led to the deterioration of food supplies and living conditions in Germany. The country had been hit by food riots and strikes in 1915. On the other hand, the countries of South America—particularly Brazil, Argentina, and Paraguay—offered a moderate climate and tolerant institutions. And many of the large cities, such as Buenos Aires, had a European feel to them.

German immigration agencies often steered their citizens to South America rather than to the United States. Germans who immigrated to the United States were frequently assimilated into local communities. By contrast, the Germans who immigrated to cities like Buenos Aires "usually settled in tight

N

0   500 mi

500 km

Caracas

GUYANA

VENEZUELA

Georgetown

Bogotá

Paramaribo

COLOMBIA

Cayenne

FRENCH GUIANA

Quito

ECUADOR

SURINAME

PERU

BRAZIL

Lima

BOLIVIA

Brasília

La Paz

Pacific Ocean

PARAGUAY

Asunción

CHILE

ARGENTINA

URUGUAY

Santiago

Buenos Aires

Montevideo

Atlantic Ocean

South America

communities and remained loyal to their cultural heritage for many generations." So when Hitler came to power, his High Command knew there were thousands of Germans in South America they could count on to advance the agenda of the Third Reich.

In fact, it was these very German enclaves in South American cities that provided sanctuary after World War II for some of the most heinous Nazi war criminals. The president of Argentina in the mid-1940s through mid-1950s, Juan Perón, "secretly ordered diplomats and intelligence officers to establish escape routes, so called 'ratlines,' through ports in Spain and Italy to smuggle thousands of former SS officers and Nazi party members out of Europe." One report claims that "an estimated nine thousand war criminals escaped to South America, including . . . other western Europeans who aided the Nazi war machine," with perhaps as many as half of them going to Argentina.

Among the war criminals who fled to South America and were captured years later was Dr. Josef Mengele, the Auschwitz "Angel of Death," who had fled to Argentina in July 1949, hiding in Buenos Aires before moving to Paraguay ten years later and then to Brazil a year later. Others of the hundreds of Nazi war criminals who found help in South America included Klaus Barbie, the former SS captain known as the "Butcher of Lyon"; Adolf Eichmann, one of the top SS officers responsible for organizing the Holocaust; Eduard Roschmann, the "Butcher of Riga," who died in Paraguay; SS Colonel Walter Rauff, creator of mobile gas chambers that killed at least one hundred thousand people; and Gustav Wagner, an SS officer simply known as "the Beast." Wagner died in Brazil in 1980, after the Brazilian federal court refused to return him to Germany to stand trial because of "inaccuracies in the paperwork."

Once the United States and England realized that a "rectification of the Treaty of Versailles would not stop Hitler's aggression and that Germany's intentions and capabilities were widely unknown," the U.S. and U.K. military intelligence agencies feared that the Germans would establish secret fuel and food supplies for their U-boats and warships along a section of the east coast of South America. The U.K. also feared that the Germans would commit acts of sabotage on British manufacturing facilities and the transportation system that supplied the U.K. with food and raw materials that it needed for its war efforts.

While none of the South American countries were active participants in World War II, U.S. leaders felt it was in the country's best interest to monitor any activities that might influence their decision to enter the war.

Lieutenant Douglas Fairbanks Jr.

Once again, Fairbanks's family connections rescued him from the mundane jobs of a typical naval reserve officer. Fairbanks still craved action, and he wasn't shy about letting his political and military contacts know of his eagerness.

In July 1942, Lord Louis Mountbatten, admiral of the fleet of the British navy and another friend of the family, invited Fairbanks to join his Combined Operations command, tasked with launching harassing raids with army and naval forces against the Germans in Europe. Mountbatten was convinced that the British should be doing more with deception. He had become especially interested in sonic deception, particularly blaring prerecorded sound of tanks and landing craft from behind smoke screens.

The Combined Operations deception project began with battlefield decoys: dummy tanks, armored cars, artillery, landing craft, and airplanes. But the dummies were only a part of the operation. Sonic trickery became a big part of the deception scheme "to give the enemy the impression of movement of an armored group." The Combined Operations tested the sounds of rolling squadrons of tanks and armored cars and added soldiers' voices and related noises. These sounds were projected from within a forest or wooded area to give the deceivers cover.

Fairbanks was stationed in Achnacarry Castle, Scotland, near Ballantrae, the "even more secret base" for deception development, where the "actual experiments with visual tactical ruses and camouflage devices were carried out." The film star did more than observe the deception practices, occasionally serving as a member of a team that cruised in a torpedo boat to test their sonic deceptions in the fog off the coast of Scotland.

After seeing the deception operations in action, Fairbanks became an "avid disciple of deception." Mountbatten wanted Fairbanks to take that passion and conviction and sell the importance of deception to the American navy.

When Fairbanks returned to the United States, he wasted no time in writing a report to Rear Admiral H. Kent Hewitt, in which he proposed a "pyramid of deception." The top layer of his scheme was a "cover and deception agency" at the highest level of the Pentagon. He further suggested a theater-wide group that would work hand in hand with the London Controlling Section. On the third level of the pyramid would be a "new, elite, amphibious combat unit" that would provide cover as the Allies invaded Europe. To move forward, Fairbanks needed to convince Admiral Ernest J. King, commander in chief of the U.S. fleet and chief of naval operations.

However, the Joint Chiefs of Staff, the body of senior U.S. military leaders, was unmoved by Fairbanks's report. As he wrote, not even the navy believed that deception operations were "anything more than a waste of time and money; they thought the idea just another set of wasteful silly tricks." What he didn't know was that two months earlier the Joint Chiefs of Staff had approved a proposal from Admiral King and General George C. Marshall, U.S. Army chief of staff, which was very similar to what Fairbanks had proposed.

Atop the JCS "pyramid" was the Joint Security Control, a high-level deception agency. At the mid-level, a theaterwide organization would coordinate with the British and would be partially filled with the Twenty-Third Headquarters Special Troops. For the third level of their pyramid, Fairbanks was given permission to form a small unit to practice deception. The amphibious units came to be known as the Beach Jumpers, whose only mission was battlefield deception, a concept the military was finally embracing.

While Fairbanks was in England learning about the deception methods of the Combined Operations, Hilton Howell Railey, an army officer with a background in journalism and public relations, was trying to advance the role of deception in the thinking of top-ranking U.S. Army minds, convinced it could "play a major role in the war."

Railey had never realized his own dream of becoming a movie actor as Fairbanks had, but he did what he could to gain a share of the national spotlight. He served in the army in World War I, then was posted in Poland as a war correspondent. He then turned to public relations, helping to organize Admiral Richard E. Byrd's Antarctic expeditions in the 1920s. It was Railey who recognized Amelia Earhart's star power and guided her rise to fame with her headline-grabbing international flights in the 1930s.

Like Fairbanks, Railey took advantage of his connections in the Roosevelt administration. In March 1941, following the start of the war, Railey contacted an army general he knew with connections in the War Department. Railey again offered his experience and expertise handling "tough jobs." He wrote that "tough jobs not only interest me but stimulate my sense of responsibility. Moreover, in this country and abroad, since 1917, I have successfully functioned as a trouble-shooter." Railey was soon activated in the army as a lieutenant colonel.

In 1942, the United States took steps to make certain it was equipped to create the weapons of victory. In September, the War Department created the National Defense Research Committee (NDRC), a group of scientists and technology innovators charged with developing new weapons. Showing its conviction in the importance of sonic deception, the NDRC created a secret section called Division 17. Railey was selected for its planning board, as was Lieutenant Douglas Fairbanks Jr., as a deception advocate and the board's naval liaison officer. Because he could write well, Railey was named secretary of the board, as well as executive officer, or second in command. The time was right for Railey and Fairbanks to meet when Fairbanks brought his fervor for deception to the planning board.

The sonic deception team had been working since February 1942 on developing a means of transmitting the sounds of an amphibious landing—including rattling anchor chains, landing-craft diesel engines, and creaking tanks—over water. The sounds of the landing would come from behind a dense smoke screen generated by quickly changing the setting on the oil-fired engines of the ships. To make the "assault" complete and realistic, high-explosive 4½-inch beach barrage rockets would be fired in the air.

The sound system that would broadcast the noise of an amphibious landing included a wire recorder (predecessor of the tape recorder) that played sounds through powerful amplifiers and monstrous 1,000-watt, twelve-horn speakers,

BEACH JUMPERS

The success of the seaborne deception at Sandy Hook legiti-
mized the use of deception for more of the military officers
who had not been fans of the tactic. And while Railey's plan for
the Twenty-Third took many months to become a reality, the
navy moved more quickly to create its own deception unit in
the Beach Jumpers, Fairbanks's brainchild.

Five months after the Battle of Sandy Hook, Fairbanks
was named commander of the Beach Jumpers and began
recruitment. He enjoyed the role of the "seasoned combat
veteran whipping the new recruits into shape" as he continued
to play the part of the dashing movie hero, crisscrossing the
country visiting college campuses looking for Beach Jumper
recruits. Notices were posted to announce that the navy was
looking for "volunteers for potentially hazardous duty, the
details of which could not be divulged in advance." The poster
attracted lots of candidates, who were told they had to meet
four basic requirements:

- No seasickness
- Experience in small-boat handling
- Enough electrical knowledge to fix a home radio
- At least fundamental knowledge of celestial navigation

Despite the success of the Battle of Sandy Hook, the army
and navy, not surprisingly, came to a parting of ways regarding

the technology of sonic deception. Fairbanks was eager to prepare his Beach Jumpers to play their role in deception operations as soon as possible. So he quickly ordered thirty sonic units like the ones used at Sandy Hook and began training his Beach Jumpers. A training base for the unit was established at Camp Bradford, Virginia, involving 180 officers and three hundred enlisted men.

The Beach Jumpers were supplied with the special equipment they would need to do their job, including wire recorders, amplifiers, 1,000-watt speakers, and gasoline generators. Later the BJs received jammer transmitters to foil enemy attempts to intercept their radio transmissions. All the equipment was loaded on sixty-three-foot Air Sea Rescue (ASR) boats, "lightly armed plywood vessels similar to the torpedo boats of the time."

After about four months of training at Bradford, the Beach Jumpers were ready for their first taste of action, receiving orders to participate in Operation HUSKY, the invasion of Sicily. On July 11, 1943, Beach Jumpers Unit 1 (BJU-1) embarked on its mission: to create a diversion off Cape San Marco, one hundred miles west of the true landing zone for HUSKY. The Allies hoped that the BJs' diversion would draw the Germans from the true invasion point. Behind a thick smoke screen laid down by the first ASR, three of the ASR sound boats played their invasion audio. By early evening, their work was completed, so the first operation of the Beach Jumpers was finished. And it was a success, as Operation HUSKY "accomplished complete surprise due to the uncertainty created in the minds of some of the German commanders" by the Beach Jumpers' deception.

Fairbanks also planned the second of the BJs' deceptions, in support of Operation ANVIL-DRAGOON, the invasion of

A high-speed patrol boat similar to those used by the Beach Jumpers

southern France in August 1944. Once the plans for the invasion were in place, the strategic "story"—the false operation that the United States wanted the Nazis to believe—was changed to suggest that the Allies no longer intended to land in southern France but "were instead planning a 'leapfrog assault' against Genoa." Fairbanks's plan called for the Beach Jumpers' convoy of assault transports and landing craft headed for the French coast to instead turn back to Arzeu, Algeria, and conduct a practice landing. German intelligence took the activity as "the onset of a new operation" and sent their forces to meet it.

One of the Beach Jumpers' jobs in preparation for the invasion of southern France was radio deception. As one of the members of that unit put it, "We poured out all kinds of commands and other information by voice during the invasion." Perhaps their most dangerous activity was to enter mined harbors to find out from fishermen where the minefields were located. The unit also made what they called a spy run, dropping three unit members posing as Italian businessmen at a small dock to gather intelligence and pick up three other "businessmen" who had completed their own fact-finding mission. Overall, the deception was another success for the Beach Jumpers. In fact, their exemplary deception ops earned them the Presidential Unit Citation.

Other BJ units in the Mediterranean took on other assignments. BJU-4, for example, assisted British commandos in the Adriatic late in 1944. They also rescued British airmen who had bailed out of disabled planes heading back to their home base after bombing Nazi oil fields in Romania.

The BJs did not have nearly as many operations as the Twenty-Third because they were limited to amphibious invasions. Nevertheless, the unit was a success. It was deactivated at war's end but was once again activated for the Korean War and saw limited action in the Vietnam War. In 1986, the BJs were renamed Fleet Tactical Deception Group and played a part in Operation DESERT STORM in 1991.

As to the origin of the name "Beach Jumpers," in 1942, Professor Harold Burris-Meyers of the Stevens Institute of Technology was placed in charge of the research for the sonic aspects of deception. When he was asked to explain the purpose of sonic deception, he replied that it was to "scare the be-jesus out of the enemy." From that time on, the success of a sonic device was measured by its "be-jesus factor," or "BJ factor." So when Real Admiral Hewitt created special small-boat deception teams, they came to be known as "BJ Teams." The name was soon changed to Beach Jumpers to match the original abbreviation.

While Rear Admiral Hewitt and Douglas Fairbanks were developing the Beach Jumpers, Colonel Railey believed that much of the equipment they were using would not meet the needs of a land-based deception team. He wanted to build a deception unit that would explore new sonic technology and develop equipment that would work for the army.

Fortunately for Railey, the Battle of Sandy Hook got the attention of the Joint Security Control. Signaling its belief in the potential importance of deception on the battlefield, the JSC moved forward with a clandestine tactical outfit. To be called the Twenty-Third Headquarters Special Troops, it would be the army's first land-based deception outfit. In addition to Railey's sonic deception unit, the Twenty-Third would include units that specialized in camouflage and signal deception. Finally, to protect the men in the outfit and maintain overall security of the unit's operations, the Twenty-Third would also include a company of combat engineers.

Now that the army had decided on the *what* of the elite deception unit, it needed to find the *who* of the unit. Where would it get eleven hundred men with the proper skills to be part of the Twenty-Third? The search wasn't easy or quick, but it gave the army exactly the blend of unconventional and highly trained soldiers that it was looking for to create the army's first organized deception unit.

called heaters. Even at moderate volume, the heaters "could blow out matches."

Always the showman, Railey wanted a dramatic demonstration of how sonic deception could shape a tactical operation. The demonstration was set for the night of October 27, 1942, at Sandy Hook, New Jersey, a three-mile stretch of beach that was designated as an island. Three hundred soldiers were to defend the beach against three hundred assault troops that would attempt to storm the area from six landing craft. Railey and other members of the NDRC planning board were to observe the attack from the deck of *Dixonia,* a yacht belonging to a pharmaceutical company owner.

What came to be called the Battle of Sandy Hook went exactly as Fairbanks, Railey, and other sonic deception supporters had hoped. Behind a smoke screen, one small boat loaded with the heater made two passes off the south end of the island, blaring the sounds of an amphibious landing. Six planes flew above the scene of the impending "battle," half laying down a smoke screen, the other half shooting flares to light the fake landing spot. At first, the commander of the troops on the island sent some of his men to investigate, but as the noise of the false invasion persisted, he ordered all his men to leave the north end of the island and head south to repel the attackers. The attacking force landed successfully, virtually unopposed on the north end of the island, demonstrating that "there might clearly be a place for sonic deception in amphibious operations."

CHAPTER 2

RECRUITMENT AND TRAINING

The creation of a command structure for the Twenty-Third Headquarters Special Troops began at the top when the army selected Colonel Harry L. Reeder to be the group's commanding officer. Reeder was a tough World War I veteran, an old tank soldier, and a career army man. Yet some officers saw this as an odd choice because they considered Reeder too narrow-minded for any outside-the-box thinking, and the concept of the deception unit was definitely outside the box for many career military men. After all, the CO and his staff were faced with a strategy that was brand-new for the army. There were no operations manuals or instruction guides for the Twenty-Third Headquarters Special Troops. To make matters more difficult for Reeder and his officers, they received no guidance or orders from the top army brass in Washington, except to prepare their troops for overseas action.

Like many officers of his generation, Reeder believed that the purpose of the army was to fight. To go into battle and outfight the enemy. Subdue him with superior tactics, weapons, and bravery. In Reeder's view, there was no room for deception in the army. He was one of the officers who believed that such tactics were somehow underhanded. Yet now he was in command of a unit whose sole purpose was to deceive the enemy. He felt there was something "sneaky and weird" about the operation and had no interest in it. He wanted to command troops in battle, not lead a fake army.

Reeder's operations and training officer, Lieutenant Colonel Clifford Simenson, shared many of his commander's feelings about the Twenty-Third. He, too, was disappointed that he was not going to the front lines to lead an infantry battalion. But while he questioned the role of deception in the army, he was far more open-minded and resourceful than Reeder. Simenson's "nimble brain [was] always at work analyzing, interpreting, judging what he heard." He was much more lighthearted and affable than Reeder, who was aloof from his troops and described by Sergeant Jim Laubheimer, one of the men in the camouflage unit, as "always kind of *harrumph*!" Simenson, on the other hand, was ready to embrace the challenge of training and shaping the Twenty-Third Headquarters Special Troops. He became "one of the prime molders" of the Twenty-Third.

Reeder and Simenson knew that the Twenty-Third would include four units, each with a different cast of characters, each with a different purpose: the 603rd Engineer Camouflage Battalion, to work with camouflage and inflatable decoys; the 3132nd Signal Service Company Special, to create and broadcast deceptive sound effects; the Signal

Company Special, to send false information for the Nazis to intercept; and the 406th Engineer Combat Company, to protect the whole unit.

They also knew that for an operation as ambitious as the Twenty-Third Headquarters Special Troops to succeed, the four units had to work as a team. Any mistake by any of the units could lead to disaster. Not only would the lives of the men in the Twenty-Third be at risk, but the soldiers in the "real" army would be imperiled if the Nazis learned, for example, that a gap in the front line was being filled not by a division of battle-hardened infantry soldiers with a full array of tanks but instead by no more than eleven hundred men armed with inflatable decoys and sound effects.

It's tempting to say that the 603rd was the most important unit in the Twenty-Third. After all, it was the largest, and it provided the visual component of the deceptions: dummy tanks and field equipment, camouflage for the dummies, and some special effects. However, the dummies would only be large inflatables without the 3132nd Signal Service Company Special's provision of the sound effects that would make them come alive in the ears of the Germans. At the same time, the work of the 603rd and the sonic unit needed to convince the Germans that the Twenty-Third was actually battalions of real soldiers moving into position for an assault. That's where the work of the Signal Company Special fit into the deception, transmitting misinformation that the Germans could easily intercept and take battlefield action upon that would play into the hands of the Allied army. In addition, with large operations, like many of those of the Twenty-Third, tough, disciplined soldiers were needed to provide protection for the others, who were, in this case, occupied with inflating dummies, setting up massive speakers, and transmitting false information, at times as close as half a mile from the German front line. That security work was the job of the 406th Combat Engineers.

All the men understood how putting themselves in harm's way, becoming "Nazi bait," was dangerous work. The Twenty-Third could only do its job successfully if the men in each unit worked together. One of the reasons the units of the Twenty-Third were able to work together so well in their deceptions was the steady influence of Frederic Fox, a young lieutenant in the Signal Company Special. Fox was "the smart guy who had a knack for coming up with the answer and making it seem like somebody else's idea." And often that "somebody else" was Simenson.

After graduating from Princeton University, Fox had gone to Hollywood to become a movie star, so he brought a theatrical flair to the operations, often taking on "the role of scriptwriter and director." As Spike Berry, one of his sergeants, recalled, "Behind every operation was a touch of Fred Fox." Fox "seemed to know just how hard to push; when to break the tension and ease off." It was no wonder that the men of the Ghost Army liked and respected him.

603rd Engineer Camouflage Battalion

Without question, the most unusual unit in the Twenty-Third Headquarters Special Troops was the 603rd Engineer Camouflage Battalion. It was the most "un-army" group of soldiers that you would expect to meet in uniform, what with its actors, artists and designers, meteorologists, set designers, and photographers all trying to create a fantasy world that would fool the Nazis and shorten the war. About half of the men in the unit were artists. The other enlisted men in the unit were, in the words of artist Arthur Shilstone, "a wild array of all kinds of people," including police officers, factory workers, supermarket clerks, and salespeople. Jack Masey recalls that the artists in the 603rd, like himself, were "looked on as kind of nutcases by the hardworking, no-nonsense backbone of America, the people who worked for a living and didn't sketch."

The backbone of the 603rd was a group of young artists who were recruited out of art schools, mostly in New York City and Philadelphia. Many of the men were students at Pratt Institute and Cooper Union, both in New York. In fact, the dean of Pratt, James Boudreau, a general in the army reserves, envisioned the importance of camouflage in a war that many people felt would leave the United States vulnerable to air attacks. Boudreau had organized a laboratory devoted to camouflage study and development. And he had also engaged camouflage experts to teach the theory and practice of camouflage at Pratt.

Recruitment for the Twenty-Third benefited from the Army Specialized Training Program (ASTP), the "single biggest college education program in the nation's history." Although the program lasted only slightly longer than a year, it sent more than two hundred thousand soldiers to more than two hundred colleges to study fields that would benefit the army, such as engineering, foreign languages, dentistry, and medicine. All soldiers selected for the program had high IQs.

However, because of the growing need for combat troops late in 1943, the army announced in February 1944 that 110,000 soldiers in the ASTP would be returned to combat duty on April 1, signaling the beginning of the end of the college program. Many of the soldiers in the ASTP had the training, education, and intelligence that the Twenty-Third was looking for in its soldiers.

For many of the men who enlisted in the army and wound up in the 603rd, it was simply a matter of patriotism to serve in the military once the United States declared war on Germany and Japan in December 1941 after the Japanese attack on Pearl Harbor. That they could serve their country while getting the opportunity to sketch and draw and paint was a bonus.

Walter Arnett, a cartoonist with the 603rd, remembered how he drilled with the unit at Fort Meade, Maryland, where they climbed trees and telephone poles, marched on "every road and by-path in the State of Maryland, [and] bivouacked on the Potomac."

All the young recruits, artists included, were also warned about the dangers of speaking to strangers who might be spies. Arnett remembers riding on the train to Fort Meade when an army major started a friendly conversation with him about where the young soldier was going and what his assignment would be. Worried that the officer was a spy, Arnett was reluctant to tell the officer anything about his orders. When they changed trains in Washington, D.C., the major helped Arnett with his bag and wished him good luck. Arnett never even told the major his name, afraid that he'd be giving away national secrets.

The artists of the 603rd were, after all, in the army and therefore expected to follow the army's rules and to complete basic training. Their commanding officer, Colonel Julian Sollohub, said that he and his staff had the sole responsibility of getting all of his men ready for combat.

And get the troops ready they did. The recruits' basic training included "lots of marching, twenty-mile hikes lugging full field packs, close-order drill with heavy 1903 Springfield rifles," and hours of calisthenics, as well as running the obstacle course: climbing over walls, "swinging on ropes across mud pits [and] crawling under barbed wire while machine gunners sprayed live ammo over their heads."

Sollohub was quite gratified with the progress of his unit. He knew that the recruits understood that, as volunteers in the 603rd, if they failed to measure up to his standards, that meant a one-way ticket to the infantry. In addition, the volunteers were motivated by a strong desire to do their best for the war effort.

When basic training was completed, the men were given "field problems," exercises cooked up by Sollohub and his staff. Some were practical engineering exercises that they might very well need to replicate when the Twenty-Third was shipped overseas. For example, the men had to build a log bridge over a creek near Chesapeake Bay. To test the construction of the bridge, the men were ordered to drive their trucks across it.

In addition, the men were ordered to erect "flattops," structures to hide vehicles and artillery. The task was hard work, beginning with sinking large, heavy poles into the soil, leaving twelve feet above ground. To support these posts, heavy wire was attached near the top of each one and then fastened to stout pegs driven into the ground with large mallets. Next, wire grids were strung across the top of the posts, like a flat roof. The wire roof on each flattop was then covered with wire mesh. Finally, strips of burlap, painted with camouflage colors, were woven through the mesh. As the men worked on their field problems, Sollohub checked the progress of each group.

While the *camoufleurs* engaged in field problems, they also took on a number of large-scale camouflage projects that were more important than training exercises. Since the fear of an attack by the Luftwaffe, the German air force, was especially keen on the East Coast of the United States, the 603rd was called upon to use its expertise to hide some important defense positions. The *camoufleurs* traveled to Long Island, New York, where they camouflaged large artillery pieces mounted on flatbed railroad cars.

At the end of 1942, the unit made a short trip from Fort Meade to Baltimore to make the huge Glenn L. Martin aircraft assembly plant invisible to Luftwaffe bombers. The plant was crucial to the war effort because it produced the B-26, a twin-engine bomber that was to become a workhorse in the air war in Europe. The size of the plant and its parking lots posed a real challenge to the men of the 603rd. The two main buildings alone covered nearly three hundred acres, equivalent to roughly 275 professional football fields. The plant was, after all, the largest aircraft manufacturer in the world during World War II, with a workforce of fifty-three thousand.

The *camoufleurs'* job was to design and create camouflage that would make the plant and its huge parking area look like regular countryside from the air. A man who was part of the 603rd saw the operation as "one of the greatest achievements in the art of camouflage."

However, after the camouflage project was successfully completed, misfortune struck. In January 1943, a severe ice

Cars parked under camouflage netting at the Glenn L. Martin aircraft plant in Baltimore

and snowstorm slammed the Northeast. Men of the 603rd, along with the 76th Infantry, were ordered to return to the plant to remove the tons of snow and ice from the camouflage nets that had collapsed on some of the sixteen thousand cars in the parking lot. While some men cleared the snow and ice from the camouflage nets, others crawled under the nets to assess the damage and take license plate numbers of the buried cars. One of the men in the detail remembered how "all the tires were flat and the tops [of the cars were] crushed in."

Victor Dowd, a painter with the 603rd, recalled that the men at Fort Meade were kept busy training. Nevertheless, the artists did have time to relax, and for them, that meant time to paint and draw. "It wasn't as if we weren't busy.

The camouflaged roof of the Boeing aircraft plant in Washington State

But . . . there's always down time." He noted that some soldiers sang and played music. Others read. Some gambled. But Dowd, and others like him, often sketched and painted in their free moments. "I just developed the habit," he said, "and I don't think it's ever left me."

Signal Company Special

For a deception plan to work, the enemy has to buy the deceivers' "story," the information that the deceivers want the enemy to believe and act on. After all, one of the goals of battlefield deception is to get the enemy to believe that something is true when it isn't, whether that's the strength of one's troops or what those troops plan to do. The 603rd was to play its part in selling the deception through visual means: camouflage, dummy tanks, and special effects. However, before enemy forces can see dummy tanks and special effects, they have to know where they are. That's the role of "spoof radio," or false and misleading radio messaging: letting the enemy learn of fake battle plans. And that task was assigned to the Signal Company Special. Sergeant Spike Berry, one of the members of the company, said one couldn't deny the importance of the "inflatable tanks or the sound guys," but they needed "a stage on which to perform. And we provided that stage."

The Allies realized that the German army relied heavily on intercepting radio transmissions to learn the enemy's plans, location of troops and equipment, and strength of their forces. In fact, it has been estimated that the German army gathered "as much as 75 percent of their intelligence from radio intercepts." The U.S. Army planned to take advantage of the German reliance on radio transmissions by feeding misinformation through the skilled hands of the radio operators of the Signal Company Special.

The U.S. Army expected that the radio transmissions sent by the Signal Company Special would be intercepted by the Nazis. In fact, the army *wanted* the messages to be intercepted because they would be filled with misinformation that would allow the Twenty-Third to fool the German army. This deception would then allow the U.S. troops to attack the Germans from an unexpected position or initiate a surprise attack.

Unlike the 603rd, which was created specifically for its

role in the Twenty-Third and trained for eighteen months at Fort Meade, Maryland, the Signal Company Special was made up of many men already in the army as members of the 244th Signal Operations Company, under the command of Captain Irwin Vander Heide. Like many soldiers who wound up in the Twenty-Third, the men of the 244th had special skills critical to the deception operation. However, not all the men of that unit were good enough to meet the needs of the Twenty-Third. The officers of the Twenty-Third were "ruthless in weeding out anyone not up to the high demands they knew would be placed on the men." In fact, "roughly 40 percent of [the men in] the 244th were transferred to other units" and never went overseas with the Twenty-Third.

The men who were accepted into the Signal Company Special of the Twenty-Third Headquarters Special Troops were selected for their ability to send and receive radio transmissions quickly using a telegraph key, much like those used in the 1830s and 1840s, the early days of the telegraph. It may seem hard to imagine in our age of instant wireless communication, but the telegraph was one of the technological advances of the Civil War. In fact, the telegraph key used by the men of the Signal Company Special was not much different from the type used by telegraphers during the Civil War.

Morse code, the language of military communications, assigned a combination of dots and dashes to all the letters of the alphabet, from A (• –) to Z (– – • •). The letters most frequently used in English words—e and t, for example—had the shortest equivalents, e being • and t being –, and no letter had more than four parts to its equivalent.

The men in the Signal Company Special sending a Morse

A typical telegraph key

code message needed a light touch on the key. When they pressed on the key, it buzzed for as long as they held their finger on it. So to send *e*, they would tap on the key for a very short signal called a dit. For *t*, they would hold the key a bit longer for a dah. They combined short and long touches to make other letters. For example, *a* would be *dit dah*, and *h* would be *dit dit dit dit.* The electrical dits and dahs would resonate across the miles to the key of the person to whom they were sending the message.

The radio operators of the Twenty-Third had to master the dits and dahs of Morse code because they were responsible for sending and receiving spoof messages on the battlefield, phony messages that they expected the Nazis to intercept. Speed and accuracy were crucial in sending messages, but also in receiving them and writing them down as they arrived in rapid-fire fashion.

The radio operators were trained to memorize the dots and dashes of the letters, but more important, to instantaneously think of the *letter* the sounds represented rather than merely hearing the dots and dashes and then taking the extra time to "translate" the sounds into a letter. Further, they were taught to master small common words, like *the, and,* and *of.* The operators needed to recognize the words they heard as *words* and not merely a string of letters. All the radio operators needed to be good listeners to detect the pattern and rhythm of messages. Finally, the radio operators of the Signal Company Special needed to transmit at a steady pace that honored the brief space between letters as well as the slightly longer space between words.

To make sure that the Germans were getting the "correct" misinformation, the radio operators of the Signal Company Special needed to follow a carefully prepared script that contained fake intelligence that the army wanted the Germans to have. The scripts changed from battle to battle, any time circumstances called for a tactical adjustment by the American command. Adhering to the script with accuracy set the stage, as Sergeant Spike Berry noted, for the actions of the 603rd and the combat engineers.

One of the men of the Signal Company Special who came to the outfit later was E. Gordon Wilson Jr. Before he was inducted into the army in 1943, Wilson worked for Western Electric as an installer of telephone equipment (long before the age of fiber-optic transmission lines and cell towers). In fact, he was on the job in Georgia when the Japanese attacked Pearl Harbor on December 7, 1941, catapulting the United States into World War II.

After he was inducted into the army, he continued to

work on telephones in Florida until he was interviewed for work with the Twenty-Third. Like all the members of the Twenty-Third, he was kept in the dark about what the new unit was all about. He recalled that he was asked one question that gave him pause: Would he rather continue to work in telephone communications or switch to radio communications? His answer, which would affect the course of his life in the army, was far from resolute. Wilson answered, "Radio—I guess." He came to realize that "the Good Lord had been with me in that decision."

His next stop was Camp Gruber, Oklahoma, where he found the Signal Company life "fairly routine, more like school." Wilson studied Morse code, learned how to assemble and disassemble a few common combat weapons, and took lots of hikes with his unit. He had been shooting guns since he was thirteen and had learned Morse code in high school, so he thought basic training was a "breeze."

Wilson and nine others from his unit were transferred to Camp Forrest, Tennessee, early in 1943, where he joined another 120 men from units all over the country who were similarly trained in high-speed radio operation. The men of the Signal Company Special trained at Camp Forrest for about five months. In addition to his communications training, Wilson was assigned to drive a two-and-a-half-ton truck that carried a huge radio transmitter enclosed in a steel shell, and also to maintain the truck and keep it and the generator supplied with gasoline.

Wilson and the men in his outfit had no idea why they had been brought to Camp Forrest. In fact, Wilson said it wasn't until fifty years after the end of the war that he realized that his unit was formed to be a secret part of the ramp-up to the invasion of France. "We were all 'shanghaied' out of other army units," he wrote, "so that there would be no record of our company being formed in order to keep it top secret."

406TH COMBAT ENGINEERS

As it did with the men of the 603rd and the 3132nd Signal Service Company Special, the U.S. Army wanted only the best-qualified soldiers for the combat engineer unit. They found what they were looking for in the 293rd Engineer Combat Battalion, and they selected Company A as "the best company of that battalion." The company had trained at part of General George Patton's sprawling and challenging desert training facility near Indio, California, and later at Camp Forrest. The legendary general would lead the U.S. Third Army from the beaches of Normandy across France to Germany.

Company A was redesignated as the 406th Engineer Combat Company and was led by Captain George Rebh, its demanding commander and one of the best students in his graduating class at West Point. In the words of one of the men of the 406th, the combat engineers were "the only real soldiers" in the Twenty-Third. Rebh made sure that his engineers could handle a machine gun as well as they handled bulldozers. The men worked on infantry tactics at night and on weekends until they had reached an acceptable level of skill. Unlike the Signal Company Special, which needed to replace many of its original units, very few of the men in the 406th failed to meet the standards set by its commander.

The unit provided security for the three other units in the Twenty-Third. They would protect the men as they did their work setting up decoy tanks, stringing radio wire, and preparing the sonic trucks. The men of the Twenty-Third often used their bulldozers to create fake tank tracks as part of a deception. Later, when the Twenty-Third moved about in populated areas of Luxembourg and France, the combat engineers also kept nosy natives from getting too close to the decoys or other equipment.

The non-fighting roles of the combat engineers included using heavy equipment to build roads and bridges for their own troops. They also constructed field fortifications and obstacles to slow the advance of enemy forces, planting land mines and digging trenches and ditches. Combat engineers also cleared enemy mines and worked with explosives to demolish structures such as bridges so the enemy could not use them.

The combat engineers brought various skills and equipment and weaponry to operations in the European theater and played a pivotal role in some of the key battles. Mechanized combat engineers guarded armored personnel carriers with a variety of heavy firepower, including demolition explosives and antitank weapons. Moving into battle, mechanized combat engineers could "unleash a tremendous amount of firepower as they established what was basically a portable minefield around the position." The light engineers moved on foot, carrying demolition supplies. The role of the heavy or topographical engineers was to provide intelligence related to mapping. One of the main roles of combat engineers was to protect friendly forces and contain attack options of the enemy.

>>>

COMBAT ENGINEERS

The *Basic Field Manual: Engineer Soldier's Handbook*, issued by the U.S. Army in 1943, spelled out what it meant to be a combat engineer:

> *You are an engineer. You are going to build bridges and blow them up. You are going to stop tanks and destroy them. You are going to build roads, airfields, and buildings. You are going to construct fortifications. You are going to fight with many kinds of weapons. You are going to make sure that our own troops move ahead against all opposition, and you are going to see to it that enemy obstacles do not interfere with our advance. You are an engineer.*

The men were "to be trained to do a man-sized job for the Army and for your country."

The use of combat engineers in the U.S. Army predated World War II. In fact, American military engineering has a long and storied history, dating to 1775, when General George Washington appointed Colonel Richard Gridley as chief engineer of the Continental Army. Four years later, Congress authorized a corps of engineers for the United States. Then called sappers or miners, they "played a significant role in

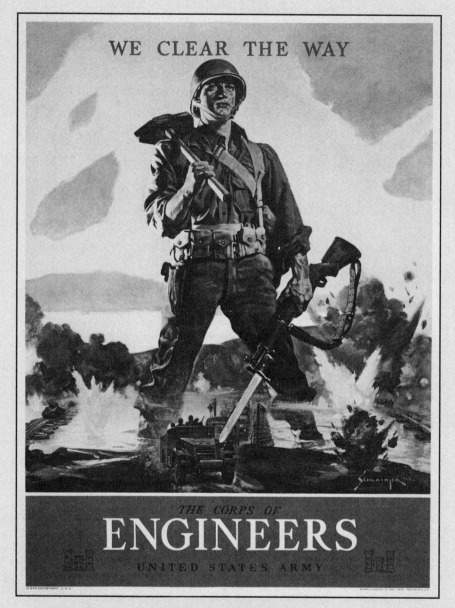

Recruitment poster for the Army Corps of Engineers

the Revolutionary War." The corps prepared defenses around strategic points, such as Bunker Hill in Boston. However, combat engineers also served a second role as fighting soldiers, a combination of duties that has continued into the present army.

In addition, the work of army engineers was not limited to the battlefield. In the early 1800s, army engineers were the driving force of the Lewis and Clark expedition to the Pacific Ocean. In the 1850s, the army engineers surveyed several routes for the proposed transcontinental railroad. And prior to the start of the Civil War, the army engineers were involved in a number of peacetime projects, playing a key role in structuring the nation's waterways and coastal shorelines, as well as working on lighthouses.

In the early weeks of the Civil War, Congress added three companies of engineers. They built field fortifications, conducted topographical reconnaissance, and constructed fixed and pontoon bridges, including a two-thousand-foot bridge across the James River in Virginia in 1864. In addition, the engineer corps "ushered in modern warfare . . . through such innovations as land mines, trench fortification and the use of balloons for observation and mapping."

Fifty years later, in World War I, the engineer corps cleared a path through No Man's Land, the area between the two front lines, suffering the first U.S. casualties of the war. In the next world war, combat engineers were among the first U.S. troops to land during the Normandy invasion, clearing concrete obstacles on the beach and in the water to prepare the way for the landing crafts that carried infantry soldiers to shore.

Once the engineers left the beaches of Normandy, they cleared and maintained roads as the Allies moved from the

French coast to Paris, and they were instrumental in turning back the Nazi attacks during the Battle of the Bulge. Wherever the engineers went, their activities were varied. They might repair and maintain buildings, clear minefields, and use explosives for demolition projects. As the manual said, they would build bridges; they would blow up bridges. They would build obstacles; they would dig trenches to deny battlefield mobility to the enemy.

However, no matter what the combat engineers were called upon to do, their objective was always the same: to change the shape of the "battle space" by giving their army the time and room to move quickly in their maneuvers.

3132ND SIGNAL SERVICE COMPANY SPECIAL

The U.S. military had begun investigating the possibility of sonic deception in February 1942, with the National Research Defense Committee's Division 17 project. The NRDC hoped that recent advances in recording and playback technology would produce benefits in battlefield deception. The military was doing what it had done with technology in the past—for example, the telegraph in the Civil War and aircraft in World War I—that is, use it to gain a tactical advantage. In 1944, after two years of training, the 3132nd Signal Service Company Special would become the fourth and final unit in the Twenty-Third.

Before the sonic unit could be part of the Twenty-Third, acoustic and sonic technicians needed to develop equipment that would succeed in the crucible of battle. With the help of scientists at Bell Labs in New Jersey, the military developed huge and powerful speakers that could project sound effects recorded on a large disk, the precursor of the vinyl record, and played on a record player. These were the "heaters," and "soon the command to start the playback became 'heat 'em up.'"

When the navy moved its sonic program from Camp Hancock, New Jersey, to Camp Bradford, Virginia, the army remained at Hancock and expanded its sonic deception operations and training at the facility. The army gave its deception operations a new name—Army Experimental Station (AES)—on June 4, 1943. With the name change came the determination that all AES work would be classified as secret.

The men of the AES worked at Hancock through the winter of 1943. But Colonel Hilton Howard Railey, the "brilliant and eccentric" commander of the Army Experimental Station, came to see that the work of the AES needed more space. To accommodate that need, he ordered the operation moved to Pine Camp in upstate New York in February 1944. With the change of location came a change of name, a change that would apply to the units of the Twenty-Third and that reflected an ever-vigilant eye on security. The terms "sonic" and "deception" were to be eliminated from all published materials or tables. Instead, the term "Special" was added to the end of the unit designations to show that these deception units were different.

Like many of the men in the Twenty-Third, notably those in the 603rd Engineer Camouflage Battalion, the men of the 3132nd Signal Service Company Special were recruited specifically to work in the secret area of deception. The commanding officer (CO) handpicked and personally interviewed every man who wound up in the AES, many of whom had been part of the Army Specialized Training Program.

Before the AES moved to Camp Pine in February 1944, it used its eighteen months at Fort Hancock very productively. Not only did the technicians reduce the weight of the heaters to forty pounds, but they also dramatically improved the quality of the sound that came from the new "baby heaters." Clearly AES benefited from the advances in sound recording. One such improvement was in the design of the speakers, which, to that point, produced very harsh sounds. The new speakers, larger and more flexible, did a better job projecting low-frequency or bass sounds, especially important for the deep sounds of rumbling tanks and large trucks.

The acoustic engineers used multichannel recording— much like the technology currently used to record music

"Heaters" mounted on a half-track

on CDs and vinyl albums. Playing back such sound effects through multiple speakers placed some yards apart gave the illusion of moving vehicles. A listener would hear "a phantom sound, a sonic illusion" that "lingered in the space between the two speakers." The engineers had also done away with the heavy and awkward batteries in favor of a portable gasoline generator as a source of electricity.

One of the reasons that the army was dissatisfied with the sound deception technology acceptable to the navy was the phonograph disks upon which the sounds were recorded. While the needle of the record player was more likely to stay in the groove of the record while a ship was sailing smoothly on the seas, the needle would bounce and skip across the record when it was jostled on a bumpy road in the back of an army truck. The army solved that particular problem by resorting to an old sound technology: the magnetic wire recorder, the precursor of the tape recorder that became popular after the war.

Since Pine Camp did not have the tanks and heavy equipment that the 3132nd needed to record for its sound effects, some of the men would have to go where the equipment was available. That meant a drive to Fort Knox, Kentucky, for Second Lieutenant Walter Manser, an "electronics geek" selected for the assignment by Railey, and eight sonic technicians. The men packed four vehicles with recording equipment and began the eight-hundred-mile drive to Fort Knox.

Railey had made sure that Manser and his technicians would have access to whatever they needed to make the necessary recordings. As Manser later reported, the commander at Fort Knox was very accommodating, providing the sonic crew with everything necessary to complete their work. And that meant a whole armored company of eighteen tanks and support vehicles, as well as nearly two hundred soldiers. Because of the "secret" designation given to anything connected with the Twenty-Third and its units, the two large maneuver fields were off-limits to all personnel not involved with the project. In addition, the army established a no-fly zone over the fields. The entire recording operation took three weeks, but Manser and his men got what they'd come for: a varied assortment of sound effects that would become an integral part of the Twenty-Third's deceptions on the battlefield.

THE ARMY HALF-TRACKS

The M3 half-tracks that served as "sonic cars" for the 3132nd Signal Service Company Special were among the forty-one thousand produced in the United States for the army in all theaters of war: North Africa, Europe, and the Pacific. As one writer noted, "No image of the American military effort in World War II is complete without the appearance of the M3 Half-Track vehicle."

The half-tracks offered advantages over the three-ton and ten-ton trucks most frequently used by the army. For one thing, they had greater mobility on different types of terrain, as well as in mud and snow. The half-track served many purposes: personnel carrier, reconnaissance vehicle, radio vehicle, ambulance, and 81mm mortar carriage. In addition, since the half-tracks had wheels in the front, they handled like trucks rather than tanks. Consequently, drivers didn't need the special training required of soldiers who drove a full-treaded vehicle like a tank.

Despite its widespread use, the half-track had its detractors because of its relatively light armor, which could not withstand machine-gun fire, and because the absence of roof protection made the vehicle vulnerable "in the face of shrapnel and air-burst shells." In fact, the half-tracks earned the infamous nickname of "Purple Heart Boxes," after the medal given to military personnel wounded or killed in combat.

The half-track originated in the woods of Maine in the early 1900s as a solution to the perennial problem faced by lumber workers: how to get logs out of the woods and to a mill. Logging railroads were often unreliable in the worst winter weather and could not be built everywhere they were needed in the woods. This was just the sort of problem that fired the imagination of Alvin Lombard, a "one-time ax-swinging Maine woodsman" whose father owned a lumber mill. He became fascinated by exploring "the 'why' of the crude appliances then used in cutting and hauling logs" and wanted to make improvements that might save both time and labor.

There had been other attempts to design and build "end-less chain drives with 'feet' or pads of wood or iron." While Benjamin Holt is "generally credited with producing the first successful crawler tractor in November 1904 . . . several others seem to have been ahead of him," including Lombard, who received a request from a local lumberman for such a machine in late 1899 or early 1900. Lombard built a wooden model of a steam-powered machine with a horizontal boiler. The machine's front was supported by a pair of sled runners. At the rear of the locomotive was a pair of endless tracks in place of large drive wheels. The machine weighed nineteen tons and could pull up to three hundred tons of logs. The prototype was first tried on Thanksgiving Day 1900, "exactly four years before Holt tested his first crawler in California."

Lombard built five such machines between 1901 and 1904, including one he sent to Colebrook, New Hampshire, where it was a sensation, pulling a long line of sleds loaded with logs. Lombard recalled, "Hundreds of thousands of people lined the road. They came from Boston and from the lumber mills in the woods, and ministers had to shut down the churches on Sunday

Lombard's crawler tractor

so people could see the event." It seems likely that Lombard was exaggerating the number of spectators, but the event was a rousing success that brought the curious to the small town. It turned out that the spectators were seeing history in "the new machine [that] revolutionized the lumber industry."

It wasn't long after Lombard's crawler became a success that the French engineer Adolphe Kégresse began producing his half-track cars. The "basic half-track concept" was applied by the British during the First World War. Between 1921 and 1937, the French army adopted the vehicles as well, as did the Polish army. The U.S. Army bought several Citröen-Kégresse vehicles for evaluation in the late twenties and developed their own design. These early half-tracks were "intended for use as prime movers or personnel carriers." The first prototype, the T7, was "the forerunner of a famous lineage, spanning seventy versions and a production of 50,000+ vehicles during World War II," including the M3, which served the men of the Twenty-Third so well.

the sound was too loud, there was a greater likelihood that the enemy would recognize it as a recording. On the other hand, if the volume was too low, the enemy would not hear the sounds. The sonic scientists worked to find the most effective volume.

In addition to all the sound equipment that the sonic half-tracks carried, they transported something else that was not standard issue on regular army half-tracks. "Under the floor were stowed packets of plastic explosives . . . arranged to assure nothing would be left" of the vehicle and equipment should the sonic car be in danger of falling into enemy hands. The detonator was accessible to the driver, and the eighteen-inch blasting fuse had a burn time of about fifteen seconds before the charge exploded. The U.S. Army was determined that its sonic equipment would remain a secret.

By the time the men of the 3132nd were ready to leave Camp Pine for the European Theater of Operations on May 30, 1944, Railey's sonic unit had produced an extensive and varied library of sound effects. It could simulate up to three battalions of many types of tanks and self-propelled artillery, moving over all sorts of terrain. The sonic men could also simulate a column of supply trucks. Not only could they play the sound of a bridge being built, but they could also simulate the sound of many different vehicles crossing that bridge. All these sounds suggested the presence of a formidable force but was really a calculated game of deadly make-believe.

CHAPTER 3

SHIPPING OUT . . .
AND MORE WAITING

The waiting was over. Or so the men of the Twenty-Third thought on April 21, 1944, when they received their orders to board a train to carry them north from Fort Meade to Camp Kilmer in New Jersey. But they spent ten days at Kilmer, where they went through "the usual . . . lectures, demonstrations and eight-hour passes to New York." As E. Gordon Wilson Jr., a member of the Signal Company Special, saw it, the troops were "always in a battle with the medics—getting shots for all kinds of foreign diseases."

On May 2, most of the troops in the Twenty-Third were on the move again. They boarded trucks with "canvas-enclosed beds and unloaded inside a huge blackout tent with only one outlet, a long canvas-enclosed walkway." The walkway led to the *Henry Gibbins,* one of seven Liberty ships delivered to the U.S. Army Transportation Corps in

1941. The *Gibbins* was nearly five hundred feet long and had a seventy-foot beam, the widest part of the hull. The units of the Twenty-Third that boarded the ship were the 603rd Engineer Camouflage Battalion, the Signal Company Special, and the 406th Combat Engineers. The men of the 3132nd Signal Service Company Special, the sound-effects team, were completing their training at Pine Camp, New York, and would not arrive in England for another six weeks.

USNS *Henry Gibbins*

The *Gibbins* was part of an enormous convoy of 150 ships, "the largest convoy ever to cross" the Atlantic. It was the last ship in the first line to starboard (right), a spot known as the "coffin corner" or "hell's corner" because the ship in that position in the convoy was frequently the first one attacked by marauding German U-boats.

According to Frederic Fox, the *Gibbins* was "a good clean ship . . . modeled after the American President luxury liners and rode well." Fox, who spent the thirteen days of the journey to England in the officers' quarters, noted that the men of the Twenty-Third "were stacked comfortably

CONVOYS

The naval convoy, which became such a crucial Allied strategy in the Atlantic, had been a common practice in the Age
of Sail (about 1550–1850), when Spain, France, and England
ruled the seas. It fell out of favor in World War I, when British
admirals thought such a cluster of ships offered a tempting
target for German submarines, or U-boats. They were also concerned about the higher risk of collisions of ships in the close
formation of a convoy. And there were some naval officers who
objected to using warships in the "defensive" way of escorting
cargo ships, rather than engaging the enemy in battle.

In the early days of World War II, however, merchant ships
and troop carriers took a terrible beating. From the start of the
war through 1942, more than twenty-six hundred ships were
hit or sunk by the U-boats. Although the United States did not
enter the war until the end of 1941, it sold tons of food and
supplies to the British, who were worried that "without the safe
arrival of the trade [the ships] carried, Britain would be unable
to continue the war." Clearly, the convoys were "created out of
desperation."

The convoys were generally categorized by their speed:
fast, medium, or slow. The fast convoys were exclusively large,
mostly British ocean liners that carried American troops to
England. Generally, the twelve or so ships in a troop convoy

would carry twenty thousand to thirty thousand soldiers as they cruised the North Atlantic at about 13 knots (15 miles per hour). The medium and slow convoys carried cargo exclusively and were more numerous, with as many as fifty ships in a slow convoy. Medium convoys traveled at about 10 knots, while the slow convoys moved at 4 to 7 knots as they crossed the Atlantic.

Before 1942, when the convoys began leaving from New York Harbor, they started from Halifax and Cape Breton, Nova Scotia. The ships met at their port of departure and sailed out of the harbor together at the same time and speed, usually in nine to eleven parallel columns, with about five ships in each. The distance across a convoy might be about eight thousand yards, about four and a half miles, with the escorts about two miles ahead of the lead line of ships. This distance gave the escorts a chance to spot U-boats before the ships came within torpedo range.

At any given time, there were "100 or more ships crossing the Atlantic from west to east, and a similar number returning"—all "timed as exactly as an express train." Each convoy sailed a different route, but each was due to arrive at a meeting spot two hundred miles west of Ireland. From there, it was usually met by nimble destroyers to escort it the rest of the way, through "the more dangerous home waters."

Convoys seldom followed the most direct route across the ocean. Rather, they usually took an "evasive course plotted in the hope of avoiding interception." Consequently, a crossing could be between three thousand and five thousand miles. The secret orders that were given to the captain of each ship, including the rendezvous point and one of the twenty possible zigzag courses, were worked out a month before leaving port.

Another strategy that the convoys used was continually changing the zigzag pattern, perhaps several times each hour. The change of pattern made it "almost hopeless to judge where the ships would be" when a U-boat would raise its periscope. The changing pattern increased the likelihood that a submarine would surface in the middle of a convoy and be blasted out of the water by the escort ships. Worse, it would be badly damaged if it collided with a ship when it surfaced.

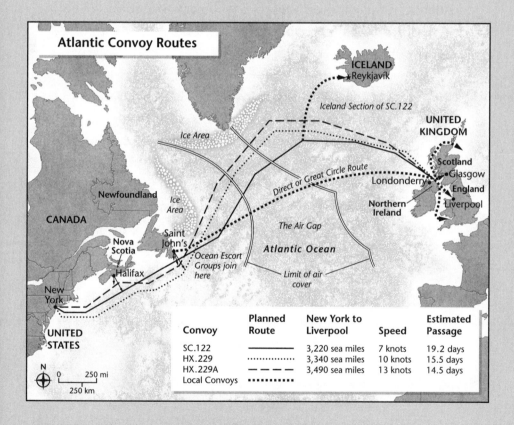

Atlantic Convoy Routes

Convoy	Planned Route	New York to Liverpool	Speed	Estimated Passage
SC.122	——————	3,220 sea miles	7 knots	19.2 days
HX.229	··············	3,340 sea miles	10 knots	15.5 days
HX.229A	– – – – –	3,490 sea miles	13 knots	14.5 days
Local Convoys	••••••••••			

When ships sailed alone, they tended to follow known shipping routes. Since there were always a number of ships at sea, U-boats would cruise the known routes and wait for a merchant ship to come into torpedo range. The skilled U-boat commanders preferred to surface and destroy the ship with the submarine's heavy deck guns. Such a practice saved torpedoes, allowing the submarine to remain at sea longer before returning to its base to load more torpedoes. The convoy changed that equation. Since a convoy was in one spot in the vast Atlantic, it was more difficult for a wolf pack of U-boats to find it. In other words, the submarine had to be in the right place at the right time.

U-boat attacks on shipping continued throughout the war, with a loss of ships and lives. However, the use of convoys with escorts, as well as the advances in submarine detection — notably the development of sonar, or underwater radar — dramatically reduced the number of ships and lives lost to the Nazis. In 1942, 1,322 ships were hit and/or sunk by U-boats. In 1943, that number was 582. It dropped by more than 50 percent in 1944 to 244. And in the first five months of 1945, before the war in Europe ended, only 98 ships were victimized by U-boats.

like sardines." Many of the troops saw their quarters quite differently. One historian described conditions as "four thousand soldiers stacked into five-high . . . berths on the airless lower decks." The men stood in chow lines for so long that they barely had time to eat before it was time get back in line for the next meal. Walter Arnett, one of the members of the camouflage unit, joked that his berth was so low in the hold of the ship that "if the Germans fired a torpedo at us it would have gone 100 feet over our heads!"

For many of the men of the Twenty-Third, the trip was their first time on a ship. E. Gordon Wilson Jr. "got sick as a dog" when the *Gibbins* was about a week out of New York. "If I wasn't seasick," he later recalled, "there were so many others sick that just being with them made me sick." Going down to the mess, "where the meals were served (and lost) would

Men packed in bunks on a Liberty ship

make you lose your appetite." Wilson never felt comfortable closed up in small places. "You can bet," he later wrote, "I didn't like having to sleep in those small, close bunks."

Ironically, the signal operator found "salvation" when the officers' mess caught fire. Fortunately, the fire was not serious, but the crew needed men to repaint the damaged mess. Ignoring the age-old advice of military life—never volunteer!—Wilson signed up for the paint crew and painted for about six nights. The perks of the job were immediate and significant: Wilson ate in the officers' mess and did not have to go to the troops' mess buried in the ship's bowels. He recalled fondly that "the cooks were friendly and loaded us up with enough food to last all day," making the remainder of the trip "almost a pleasure cruise."

When the weather was good enough to see anything, the men could spot nothing but ships stretching across the Atlantic. The artists in the 603rd tried to spend as much of the long journey as possible on deck, sketching, drawing, and painting. Among other things, the men "drew figure studies of the other soldiers, tableaux of sailors at the guns, seascapes of ships passing around them." Those artists who trained at Pratt Institute remembered the instructors who told them that they had to continue their work: "Wherever we go, whatever we do—be an artist." The artists followed that advice when they were at Fort Meade and continued that practice for the rest of the war. A number of them captured on paper the magnificent *Queen Mary*, pressed into service as a troop transport, as she sailed past, fairly close to the convoy. The men learned that the *Queen Mary* never traveled as part of a convoy. She was too fast as she zigzagged across the Atlantic to elude the U-boats.

〉〉

LIBERTY SHIPS

At the outbreak of World War II, American leaders realized that if England was to escape the clutches of Hitler's war machine, it would need help. While the United States was months away from committing troops to fight the Nazis, it could provide the British with food and war supplies. President Roosevelt decided that the U.S. shipyards needed to build merchant ships at a rate like never before, and they needed to start immediately. With the formation of the U.S. Maritime Commission under the Merchant Marine Act of 1936, the United States began a program to launch an enormous fleet of merchant ships. So it was that the famous Liberty ships were born.

American shipbuilders utilized the assembly-line process, which would allow the ships to be launched more quickly and at a lower cost than their British counterparts. Each ship contained more than thirty thousand components and prefabricated sections, "produced in thousands of factories in more than thirty-two states" and transported to the eighteen shipyards that were building Liberty ships. Each of the "cookie-cutter" ships was about 450 feet long and 60 feet wide. The ships managed a top speed of 11 knots, about 12½ miles per hour, and had a range of seventeen thousand miles. Each Liberty ship carried a crew of "between 38 and 62 civilian

A typical Liberty ship

merchant sailors, and 21 to 40 naval personnel to operate defensive guns and communications equipment."

Although 2,710 Liberty ships were built to carry supplies to England, 225 of them were later retrofitted to carry troops. On each ship, two of the forward cargo holds were converted to accommodate 350 bunks. As the demands for troops rose, the space was further changed to hold 550 bunks, stacked four or five high. "The galley and mess facilities were very unsatisfactory. The sanitary installations were inadequate. . . . Ventilation and heating were poor." One marine historian describes the conversions as "crude," noting as well that "these barely livable spaces were often filled to over capacity."

Later, two hundred Liberty ships were part of the D-day invasion.

The *Gibbins* eased into the Bristol Channel on May 15, 1944. As the ship approached Bristol Harbor, the sky was ablaze with lights from the gigantic spotlights that tried to pin Luftwaffe bombers in the sky so they could be shot down by British antiaircraft fire. The men of the Twenty-Third remained onboard the *Gibbins* until the bombing raid had run its course and the enemy planes fled to their airfields.

Reeder, Simenson, and the other staff officers who had flown over earlier were on the pier to meet the troops. The men were ordered to grab their gear and board the London Midland and Scottish Railway train that would be their means of transportation for the next seven hours as it carried them seventy-five miles northeast to their bivouac near Stratford-upon-Avon (the birthplace of William Shakespeare). The men of the Twenty-Third still had no idea what their mission was. They were, of course, in the dark about Operation BODYGUARD (1944), the code name for the enormous and

A Liberty ship being unloaded in England

complicated deception plan for the D-day invasion, which was three weeks away.

When the men arrived at Stratford, their journey wasn't quite over. They piled on trucks and were driven five miles farther to Walton Hall, a sumptuous estate belonging to Lady Harriet Mordaunt, who had agreed to let the British military use the grounds as a bivouac area. The troops came to call the main building "the Castle." Not that any of them were to live there. That, of course, was reserved for the officers, who nicknamed it "Moldy Manor." The troops were billeted on the manor's carefully manicured grounds, which included

Walton Hall, aka Moldy Manor

forests and a swan lake as well as stables, a coach house, barns, worker cottages, and a graveyard. Some of the troops lived in tin-roofed Nissen huts, or Quonset huts, as they were known in the United States. Most of the men, however, lived in canvas tents in the meadow near the main road to the manor.

The code name given to the Twenty-Third while it was in England was ARIZONA. However, in the summer of 1944, after the entire unit was working in Europe, the name was inexplicably changed to BLARNEY, a name that could be seen as a serious violation of security because it could easily give away the purpose of the Twenty-Third. Regardless of the reason, the name stuck, and the 603rd was BLARNEY RED, the 406th was BLARNEY WHITE, the 3132nd was BLARNEY BLUE, and the Twenty-Third was BLARNEY ORANGE.

The first order of business for the unit was to gather their equipment, which had been shipped to the U.K. and was stored in huge warehouses across southern England. One of the men responsible for taking inventory of the equipment and shipping it to Walton Hall was Walter Arnett, a cartoonist in the 603rd. He received secret orders to travel to Swansea, a city on the south coast of Wales.

Arnett's mission was to check every crate for special equipment earmarked for the Twenty-Third. Such equipment was loaded on a freight train and bound for "Honeybourne," the code name for the camp at Walton Hall, which was derived from the name of the nearby town of Wellesbourne, about two miles east of the estate.

At the end of each day, in a "cloak and dagger fashion," Arnett called London from a pay phone in Swansea to speak to a "Colonel Rapwatt," a man on the London staff of General

Camoufleurs unpacking a tank decoy

A decoy tank ready to fool the Nazis

or deflated in a matter of minutes." Once the dummies were in position, the men constructed camouflage around them.

Hitler believed that an invasion of France would fail if he could repel the invaders even for a day or two. For their part, the Allies realized that the success of the invasion, perhaps even the outcome of the war in Europe, was tied to fooling Hitler about the time and the location of the invasion. Operation BODYGUARD was the most complicated battlefield deception in modern times.

BODYGUARD had three main objectives. The most important objective was to make Hitler believe that the point of invasion was Pas-de-Calais, about two hundred miles northeast of the real invasion site along the Normandy coast. If the Allies could fool Hitler into believing their forces would come ashore at Pas-de-Calais, they had a good chance of achieving their second objective: getting Hitler to keep a large number of troops and tanks in that area until it was too late for him to order them to the real invasion site. The third objective of BODYGUARD was to keep secret the real date, time, and place of the invasion. BODYGUARD was a gigantic jigsaw puzzle with many interlocking deception operations, but its main operations were FORTITUDE NORTH (1944), aimed at keeping a quarter of a million Nazi troops in Norway, and FORTITUDE SOUTH (1944), which would concentrate on the invasion of France.

A deception like BODYGUARD, as well as some of the operations that the Twenty-Third would begin shortly after they landed in Normandy, was known as a "force multiplier." Obviously, the operation would not actually increase the number of troops the Allies had at their disposal. However, by making it seem as if the Allied forces were going to attack at a number of places along the Nazis' sixteen-hundred-mile so-called Atlantic Wall, they would force Hitler to spread out his troops and tanks to counter all the possible points of attack, making the German forces vulnerable to assaults at any of the places. And if Hitler kept his troops in Pas-de-Calais, they would be unable to offer reinforcements to the places the Allies actually attacked. However, to create a credible deception, the Allies needed to fabricate notional, or fake, armies that the Nazis would believe were real. This was what the deception masterminds did when they created FORTITUDE NORTH and FORTITUDE SOUTH.

The "story" of FORTITUDE NORTH was that the Allies were planning to invade Norway. Allied intelligence believed that because Hitler relied on Norwegian iron ore for his armies, he would do whatever it took to maintain control of the country. FORTITUDE NORTH would take advantage of this information and use it against Hitler. At the time the Allies were preparing to invade France, the Nazis had nearly a quarter of a million troops stationed in Norway, in addition to a large Luftwaffe presence and a Panzer (tank) division. The Allies saw that as more than twice the number of troops needed to control the people of Norway. The Allies realized how important it could be for the coming invasion if they could convince Hitler to keep his 250,000 troops in Norway. To that end, they created Operation FORTITUDE NORTH.

Both FORTITUDE NORTH and FORTITUDE SOUTH relied on the physical deception of dummies, decoys, and camouflage, practices that the Twenty-Third would use on European battlefields. And as Britain's Royal Air Force controlled the skies over the British Isles since its victory in the Battle of Britain in 1940, it only let Luftwaffe reconnaissance planes fly over England when it served its purpose—for example, so they could see and be fooled by the wooden and inflatable tanks, trucks, and fighter planes. Such flights allowed the Germans to confirm misinformation that the Allied radio signalmen had been filling the airwaves with and allowing the Germans to intercept and decipher.

The heart of FORTITUDE NORTH was the notional army that was created by the Allies to show the Nazis that they were preparing for an invasion of Norway. At the start of the operation, the notional Fourth Army was a blend of real and fake troops in Scotland. However, the army was only a few hundred men from the Twenty-Third, wildly driving around different parts of Scotland with their signal equipment, sending out countless messages to simulate a much larger army. The success of FORTITUDE NORTH neutralized Hitler's valuable resources, removing them as a threat to the Allies hitting the beaches of Normandy.

FORTITUDE SOUTH was a much more ambitious deception than FORTITUDE NORTH. It was also considerably more important since it was created to conceal the actual invasion of France. It was designed to convince Hitler to keep his Seventh Army and his fierce Panzer divisions near Pas-de-Calais for even just a couple of days. The Allies were betting that the extra time might be enough for them to gain a foothold in France and begin their march to Berlin to crush Hitler's Third Reich.

Hitler and many of his generals were already predisposed to believe that the invasion would come at Pas-de-Calais because it made strategic sense for the Allies to attack there. For one thing, the distance between Dover, England, and the French city was only twenty miles, the shortest distance between the two countries, allowing RAF fighter escort planes to provide air coverage for the landing craft of the invasion. The short distance also allowed landing craft and supply ships to make several daily trips between Dover and Pas-de-Calais. And the French city offered a deep-water harbor that would suit the larger Allied ships that would supply support for the troops.

Another reason the execution of FORTITUDE SOUTH was so tricky was that the operation needed to accomplish two very different things. The southern coast of England was roughly divided into two sections, with Portsmouth at the center: the southeast coast included the area east to Dover; the southwest coast west to Exeter, including the area from which the D-day invasion would launch. So the Allies had to convince the Nazis that the First United States Army Group (FUSAG) activity around Dover and the East Anglia region, north of Dover on England's east coast, was real, while at the same time hiding the nearly one million soldiers and support personnel that were preparing to sail for Normandy out of the Portsmouth area on England's south coast.

The camp for the notional FUSAG was an elaborate masquerade of fake aircraft, tanks, heavy equipment, and artillery created by designers, painters, and artists brought in from London-area movie studios to fool Nazi aerial reconnaissance flights. The camp was a sprawling area of large tent cities and dirt roads leading into nearby woods to give the appearance of roads to ammo depots or other areas the Allies wanted the Nazis to think were secret.

Of course, large areas of tents by themselves would not be enough to fool the Nazis' air reconnaissance analysts. So other facilities needed to be built by the small army of

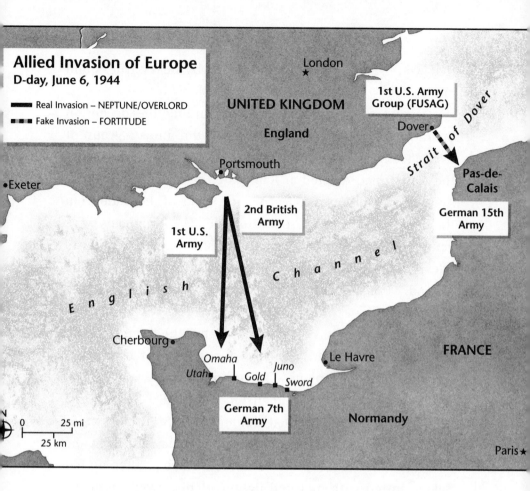

London ★

UNITED KINGDOM

England

1st U.S. Army Group (FUSAG)

Dover •

Strait of Dover

Portsmouth

• Exeter

Pas-de-Calais

2nd British Army

German 15th Army

1st U.S. Army

E n g l i s h   C h a n n e l

Cherbourg •

FRANCE

Omaha
Utah   Gold   Juno   Sword
• Le Havre

N
0   25 mi
25 km

German 7th Army

Normandy

Paris ★

British *camoufleurs* and carpenters; these included dining halls, ammo depots, and medical facilities, in addition to a parking area lined with all manner of mostly fabric-and-wood military vehicles, including ambulances. And since the Nazi intelligence analysts would not be fooled by rows of vehicles that remained in one spot day after day, the Brits moved many of the vehicles, always under cover of night, lest the reconnaissance flights spotted soldiers carrying the lightweight fake vehicles to a new spot. As a finishing touch, the deception team designed special tire-and-tread devices that left plenty of marks on the roads and in the fields that would look like the imprints left by heavy trucks and tanks.

Despite the tight security surrounding the deception operations of BODYGUARD, the Allies did allow a group of five officers of the Twenty-Third to inspect a decoy site that the British had created at Ramsgate, near Canterbury. The Americans had hoped to learn some tricks of the trade from the more experienced British. However, the Americans were generally disappointed by what they saw. The British efforts had produced "a phantom but static army on their home ground." Consequently, their dummies looked crude and primitive.

It seemed to the visiting officers that the dummies they saw were not as sturdy or as realistic as their own counterparts. The fake planes, for example, were made from wood and looked one-dimensional. The British assured the Americans that the "flat dummy Spitfire aircraft made of painted plywood appeared three-dimensional from the air." The Americans wondered how runways painted on flat fields, dotted with plywood fighter planes, would fool the Nazis, but, in fact, such dummy installations frequently drew Luftwaffe attacks.

The British also disguised hangars filled with real fighter planes as quaint cottages, "complete with chimneys and gables and half-frame timbers painted on metal." While it was true that from a few hundred yards they still looked like hangars, the British assured the Americans that they looked genuine enough from the air. The British told their American counterparts that "it was hard for a pilot to judge scale without something to which these cottage hangars could be compared." In other words, if there were no cars and trucks near these fake cottages, for example, it was difficult for an aerial reconnaissance crew to tell how large they really were. To avoid housing too many planes in one place, where they could be vulnerable to German bombers, the British dispersed them among numerous cottage-hangars across the countryside.

While the officers of the Twenty-Third found the British dummies and deception equipment unsophisticated compared to their own, it was something of an unfair comparison. The Americans had created a deception unit that needed to be fluid and mobile. Although the men of the Twenty-Third didn't know it when they were in England, they would be moving through France, Luxembourg, Belgium, and Germany, from battle to battle, needing to be ready to adjust to whatever the Nazis threw at them, while the British needed to create scenes that would look realistic to German aerial surveillance.

The Americans did, in fact, learn some useful techniques from the British, techniques the British had used in their successful deception operation in the African desert at the Battle of El Alamein. For example, the British showed how two artillery pieces could be positioned facing each other with their wheels visible, then covered with a light-weight frame and olive-drab canvas to look like a jeep or small truck. The American officers also learned the common British practice of storing fuel or other supplies under cover in the shape of a small vehicle. Such "vehicles," which might seem too small a target for German air attack, could actually hide tons of food or gasoline.

The men of the 603rd knew they needed to make sure their decoys were more realistic than the ones the British made. Each decoy was inflated a second time, confirming that none had leaks. If the decoys held air, they were carried to another field, where they sat a while longer to make sure they had no leaks. Those decoys that passed the test were "carefully packed in canvas cases and labeled with the type of replica it held." When deflated and stored in their canvas storage bags, fifteen to twenty dummies could fit in a typical two-and-a-half-ton truck.

Although the decoys were often called "rubber inflatables," they were not made of rubber at all, and were more than just large balloons like the ones in holiday parades. The decoys were, in fact, made of neoprene, a synthetic rubber fabric that was more durable than rubber, especially in the extreme conditions that the decoys would need to endure. (A modern version of neoprene is used in scuba-diving and surfing wet suits.) The rubber fabric was "stretched over air-filled neoprene tubes, which gave the dummy shape and rigidity." If one of the tubes sprang a leak, it was easy to replace that single tube instead of the entire dummy.

Once the *camoufleurs* were convinced that the decoys would stay inflated, the dummies were moved to a painting station and painted either olive drab or a camouflage pattern. Finally, a white star of the U.S. Army was stenciled on each piece of fake equipment. Since the dummies were part of a visual deception, they needed to look realistic because, as a source of misinformation, they were *meant* to be spotted by the enemy.

As a finishing touch, the *camoufleurs* made sure that each decoy had tabs on the bottom so it could be fastened to the ground with long spikes to prevent it from tipping over or blowing away in strong winds. The Twenty-Third wanted to avoid the near disaster that the British experienced when large inflatable landing craft set up in the water near Dover blew about in high winds. Fortunately, that problem was corrected before the Luftwaffe spotted the windblown landing crafts.

In addition to the work that the men of the 603rd did making sure their inflatable dummies were ready for battle, they participated in three field exercises in Thetford Forest, about 110 miles east of Walton Hall. Each exercise lasted about two days, between May 29 and June 3, 1944, and was something of a dress rehearsal for real operations in France. However, they were quite limited in that none of the exercises involved the radio, sonic, or special effects of the Twenty-Third, so they didn't do much to improve the Twenty-Third's techniques.

An inflatable landing craft

An inflatable troop carrier

The first exercise, with the code name of CABBAGE, involved elements of visual deception—that is, inflatable dummies and constructed decoys—to simulate a single armored division (between ten thousand and fifteen thousand men). The second practice exercise was called CHEESE and took place on May 31 to June 1. It followed the same action plan as CABBAGE. The final field exercise, SPAM, which took place on June 2–3, simulated a notional infantry division.

Were these limited field exercises helpful? Allied Command was looking at the big picture: How did the units with their fake tanks and artillery look in the bivouac area or as a combat unit? One World War II historian wrote that, although he found "no after-action reports," the exercises "appear to have been a worthwhile shakedown for the troops."

While the radio operators of the Signal Company Special did not actually participate in the six days of field exercises, they were nonetheless quite busy. Since most radio transmissions from army units larger than a battalion (five hundred to eight hundred soldiers) used Morse code rather than oral transmissions on a field telephone, the radiomen needed to spend long hours during the week of exercises learning what kinds of transmissions were sent by units of various types and sizes. For example, what type of messages would an armored division send? How might they be different from the messages sent by an infantry division?

In addition, the radiomen of the Twenty-Third needed to learn to duplicate the "fist" of the sender, since each sender had a different touch and rhythm when transmitting messages. A sudden and significant change in the way Morse code messages were transmitted by Allied signalmen would quickly raise red flags for Nazi intelligence.

Nearly a month after three of the four units of the Twenty-Third arrived in England, the 3132nd Signal Service Company Special, the sonic unit that had been training at Pine Camp in upstate New York, walked off the SS *Exceller* in Scotland's Glasgow Harbor on June 10, 1944. Along with the men came a convoy of vehicles: eighteen sonic cars, those customized half-tracks packed with sonic equipment covered by tarps, and an assortment of jeeps and trucks. Men and equipment were loaded on a train for the three-hundred-mile trip to the green fields of Moldy Manor, where, for a few weeks, the soldiers of the 3132nd "enjoyed the diversions of [the area] in between more practical practice sessions with their equipment" as they fine-tuned their skills for the battlefields of France.

While the men of the Twenty-Third waited for what would come next, a group of thirteen radiomen under the command of Lieutenant Fox had been selected to be part of the "first mission to fall under Twenty-Third control" in France. With a handful of jeeps and trucks, the men joined the Ninth Infantry Division in Wales, which later joined the Eighty-Seventh Armored Field Artillery Battalion's Operation TROUTFLY as part of Task Force HOWELL. After landing on Utah Beach in Normandy, the Eighty-Seventh was to reinforce the Eighty-Second Airborne Division the day after D-day.

Those taking part in the deception paid special attention to the small things to "sell" their deception. The men in the operation even wore Ninth Infantry Division shoulder patches and had memorized the names of the units as well as the officers of the division. And all the vehicles bore the markings of the Ninth, just in case German spies were watching.

The radiomen were prepared to send spoof messages in an attempt to fool the Nazis into believing that the Ninth was merely taking a defensive position in "an area where the Americans would, in fact, be very weak." The truth at the core of TROUTFLY was that the Ninth, as reinforcement for the Eighty-Second, was an offensive army that would move into France with the Eighty-Second Airborne.

Despite all the planning, the operation seemed doomed from the start when their Liberty ship, USS *John S. Mosby,* sailed to the wrong Normandy beach. But that was only the beginning of the operation's ill fortune. The *Mosby* made it to Utah Beach on the evening of June 7, but two other ships in the convoy didn't. One was blasted by a five-hundred-pound bomb and sank. Another hit a mine. In the confusion of the invasion site, "Allied ships twice rammed the *Mosby* accidentally . . . and two members of TROUTFLY . . . were wounded by falling [antiaircraft] flak during an air alert."

The men involved in TROUTFLY finally got ashore on June 10, four days after D-day, but the landing got them no closer to their goal. Their mission continued to be plagued by bad luck when the Eighty-Second lost nearly all of its equipment in their airborne landing on D-day. Since the Eighty-Second couldn't proceed without radio communication, TROUTFLY was chosen to be the radio unit for the division. The radiomen provided the Eighty-Second with its communication link to headquarters in England and with divisional headquarters, but the men of TROUTFLY never participated in a deception that utilized their special training. Ten days after D-day, TROUTFLY was released from its duty with the Eighty-Second and ordered to assist with signals intelligence monitoring for the First Army at Omaha Beach.

On June 24, 1944, when the remainder of the Twenty-Third arrived in France, they were reunited with the members of the unit that were part of TROUTFLY. Together, they would begin their journey across Europe that would see them execute deceptions in some of the most ferocious battles of World War II.

CHAPTER 4

THE TWENTY-THIRD GETS INTO ACTION

On June 16, 1944, ten days after the invasion of France began, Colonel Reeder and about 35 percent of all the men in the Twenty-Third (40 officers, 319 troops) made the crossing from England to Omaha Beach in Normandy. This smaller unit was code-named ELEPHANT, which would also be the name of its operation in France (July 1–4). The members of the unit that remained in England (34 officers, 563 troops), "officially called RESIDUE or informally, 'Garbage,'" would not leave for France until July 8.

The Twenty-Third's first deception operation hit a snag soon after the unit left Walton Hall when it was misdirected to Exeter, where the men spent two nights in the fields of Bishops Court, a country estate. On June 18, they were rerouted east to a camp near Southampton. The next day, they boarded two landing craft, LSTs 284 and 335, to cross the channel. However, LST 284 dropped out of the convoy and anchored off the Isle of Wight for a week. Lieutenant Fox reported that "no one cared because the ship was very comfortable and the weather, perfect." The men enjoyed movies that were shown on the tank deck. Hot bread and butter and coffee were served each night. The men seemed "more curious than frightful." While LST 284 sat at anchor, LST 335 landed on Omaha Beach on June 24. Three days later, 284 landed.

The D-day landing on the beaches of Normandy had been a massive undertaking. During the night of June 5, 1944, more than five thousand ships moved to their assigned positions in the English Channel. Early the next morning, nearly fifty thousand U.S. troops rushed ashore, under Nazi fire from cliffs high above the beach. As good as the Allies'

At Sea on an LCI (Landing Craft, Infantry), a watercolor by Edward Ardizzone

A view of part of the Normandy invasion force

pre-invasion intelligence was, it had overlooked these enemy positions. The fighting continued as the Twenty-Third landed on Omaha Beach.

The invasion was a success, and the beachhead was eventually secure. Nevertheless, the Allied troops made

American troops in England prior to D-day

little progress breaking out of Normandy and moving deeper into France until late in July. The troops "remained wedged within a narrow bridgehead roughly fifty miles wide and twenty miles deep." The fighting to move beyond the beach was "intense, grim, and unspeakably violent, with daily advances limited to a few yards."

While Fox believed the men were more curious than frightful as they waited offshore in the LST, no doubt that equation changed when the members of the Twenty-Third hit Omaha Beach. The Twenty-Third was about to stage a production like no other. There had been deception operations by the British earlier in the war, but the work of the Twenty-Third would combine visual and spoof radio with sonic deception. The Twenty-Third had never experienced setting up a deception operation in the chaos of battle, and they had never experienced life and death on the battlefield. All in all, there was ample cause for "opening-night jitters" as they piled out of their LSTs and raced up Omaha Beach into Nazi fire.

Prior to their departure, the men of the Twenty-Third were ordered to turn in the gas masks, which they had "carried everywhere for nearly two years." The men received no explanation for the change. On the other hand, the artists of the 603rd were allowed to retain their art kits, which included pens and ink, paints and brushes, and pencils and paper. Arthur Shilstone recalls that he and his fellow artists did art "to keep from going crazy. It was just so automatic, like writing or talking."

The artists among the Twenty-Third had plenty of opportunities to capture the horrific scenes of war, starting with the short but dangerous drive to their first mission.

》》》

FROM HOLLYWOOD TO THE BATTLEFIELD: FREDERIC FOX

When Frederic Fox was a student at Princeton University, he wanted to be a Hollywood star. He had been a member of the Triangle Club, the "oldest collegiate musical-comedy troupe in the nation." Fox starred in musicals that toured East Coast cities "to great acclaim." So, after graduating college in 1939, Fox went to Hollywood, hoping for the big chance that would make him a movie star. He had no such luck, settling for a number of writing jobs, like composing ad copy for a popular baby food and an in-house newsletter for NBC Radio.

Fox enlisted in the army following the Japanese attack on Pearl Harbor. The army must have seen promise in the tall and lanky young man who "looked like a young assistant professor of English," because they selected him for Officer Candidate School. It was some time after he graduated from OCS as a lieutenant that he was able to put his skills to work in the Twenty-Third Headquarters Special Troops, writing scripts for the deception operations and staging the actions of the unit, "passionately" urging his men to take "a more theatrical approach to their deceptions." Despite his hand in making the deceptions more theatrical, Fox was more than just a stage director. He was a soldier, discharged with the rank of captain and with a Bronze Star and five battle stars to his credit.

After the war, Fox studied at Union Theological Seminary

in New York and served as a Congregational minister in churches across the country from Washington, D.C., to Arizona. In 1956, he joined the staff of President Eisenhower, the former Supreme Commander of Allied Troops in the European Theater of Operations, where he put his writing skills to work again. This time he helped write presidential speeches and proclamations, as well as drafted replies to letters sent to the president.

Lieutenant Frederic Fox

During his time as a writer for Eisenhower, Fox tried to get the army to declassify the records of the Twenty-Third so he could write a book about the unit. He did write the "Official History of the 23rd Headquarters Special Troops," but it was not declassified during Fox's lifetime.

When Fox left the Eisenhower White House in 1961, he taught journalism to African church leaders in what was then Rhodesia (now Zimbabwe) and wrote about his experiences in *14 Africans vs. One American.* Fox ultimately returned to Princeton, where he preached an occasional sermon. After he died, in 1981, his ashes were buried under the university chapel.

American soldiers on Omaha Beach recovering fallen comrades after the D-day invasion

Harold Laynor, "simultaneously dazzled by the French countryside and appalled at the destruction in every field and village," had dreamed of roaming the French landscape and capturing the splendor of its scenes on canvas and paper. Instead, the scene included the devastated remains of an American armored column that had been ambushed in a hedgerow and decimated by Nazi antitank guns and machine guns.

With such scenes fresh in their minds, the Twenty-Third moved on to the Forest of Cerisy, a dozen miles from their landing site on Omaha Beach and ten miles from the pivotal crossroads of Saint-Lô, which was one of several German strongholds blocking the Allied breakout from the Normandy beach. U.S. bombers had been relentlessly pounding the area, but the Nazis remained dug in. The Twenty-Third would be part of the Allied plan to drive the Nazis from Normandy.

For its first operation, the Twenty-Third was divided into three units, each with different responsibilities. Combat Command A (CCA) would simulate two armored regiments (two thousand to four thousand men in each) and two armored infantry battalions (three hundred to eight hundred men in each). The CCA would use 140 decoy vehicles. Combat Command Reserve (CCR) would simulate two

Four GIs move a tank decoy.

armored regiments and one infantry battalion. This command would use ninety-seven inflatable decoys. The last of the units was Combat Command B (CCB), simulating two armored field artillery battalions while deploying one hundred rubber decoys and fifty-eight camouflage nets. Bear in mind that the Twenty-Third involved in ELEPHANT was not at full strength. There was only one spoof radio team in their operation, and the sonic unit was still in England.

The Twenty-Third's mission was to cover the Second Armored Division when it moved out of its reserve position to take up its new position in the line between the First U.S. and Second Canadian Armies. On July 1, as the tanks of the Second Armored Division began rumbling out of the forest, the men of the Twenty-Third began to replace the tanks with their inflatables.

When the Twenty-Third set up their tank decoys, they learned a valuable lesson about security. A French farmer wandered up to one of the fake tanks and touched it before anyone could stop him. We can imagine his surprise when he realized the tank was an inflatable decoy. A smile spread across the farmer's face "as he slowly touched his finger to his forehead and said 'Ah, boom-boom—ha ha!'"

While the farmer was amused by the dummy tanks, Lieutenant Colonel John W. Mayo, in command of CCB, was not amused in the least. Though the farmer turned out to be a friendly "local," that incident led to several recommendations for changes in the security surrounding all decoy sites. Mayo wanted more men involved in the security at each site. In addition, he felt that setting up decoys no closer than six hundred feet from roads would afford a buffer zone to deter wandering locals—be they friendly or enemy agent—from

Arthur Shilstone's painting of two Frenchmen looking on as GIs move a tank decoy

getting too close to the decoys. He further suggested that a counterintelligence agent who spoke French accompany the unit when it arrived in an area to set up a new decoy operation.

One of the problems with ELEPHANT was that the tanks in the Second Armored moved only four miles away, too close to the decoys set up by the Twenty-Third. To make matters worse, the Second fired its guns at the German positions and sent some of its infantry into the line, in a sense announcing its presence a short distance from the Twenty-Third. It was clear to Fox that the Second had been identified by the Nazis, defeating the whole purpose of the deception operation, which was to let the real unit move off and attack the enemy from a more advantageous position.

To make the decoys even more vulnerable, the tank drivers began pulling out of the bivouac area an hour after the Twenty-Third arrived, giving the unit little time to set up its decoys. In addition, the Second, having no idea of the deception plan, left significant tread marks in the area that would be clearly visible to German reconnaissance planes. The departing tanks traveled by day, with no thought to the cover that darkness would have given their movement. The commander of the Twenty-Third would have preferred that the Second moved a handful of tanks at a time at night.

An American aerial reconnaissance plane that flew over the work the Twenty-Third had done noted an obvious lack of action in the area. The flyover also reported that there were too few inflatable decoys and camouflage nets for a division of at least ten thousand troops and support personnel. To make the deception area look more realistic, the aerial team suggested parking real vehicles camouflaged just enough so they could be recognized by German aerial surveillance planes. They also suggested having white clothes near the dummies to give the appearance of wash on the line.

Ironically, one of the criticisms of the operation was that the *camoufleurs* of the 603rd had done their job too well. The camouflage was *too good.* After all, if the vehicles were too well hidden, the Germans wouldn't spot them. As a result, the men of the 603rd were instructed to make "camouflage mistakes," giving the Nazis the chance to spot some of the dummy tanks and artillery pieces. "One third of the mistakes should be minor ones, one third medium, and the final third would be severe, or very poor camouflage jobs."

Another problem discovered in ELEPHANT was the way the Twenty-Third's equipment had been loaded on the transport ships in England. The equipment had been packed in the order it was thought it would be used. This turned out to be a problem when the equipment needed early in ELEPHANT was buried behind supplies that wouldn't be required until later. This problem was resolved when the equipment the men needed to begin an operation was packed on the ships last. This meant that the equipment needed to set up an operation would be unloaded first and trucked to the operation site, while subsequent trucks brought equipment that wouldn't be used until later in the operation.

On July 3, tanks and artillery from the Third Armored Division began to move into the area where the Twenty-Third had established its fake operation. With the arrival of the Third, the work of the Twenty-Third was finished, and the unit "faded out" on July 4.

After the fade-out, the officers of the Twenty-Third began to assess the unit's efforts, something they would do after each of the operations. Was ELEPHANT a success? A more important question became part of their evaluation of each operation: How could the Twenty-Third make it better? The answer to the first question was obvious to the officers of the unit. As Lieutenant Fox reported following ELEPHANT, "There is every reason to suspect . . . that little good was done." Although the operation did little to help the Second Armored Division or the American and British armies that it was serving, it was of "considerable help" to the Twenty-Third as a training experience.

But the bulk of the changes in store for the Twenty-Third's operations were enumerated in a memo written a week after their ELEPHANT fade-out. According to historian Jonathan Gawne, the draft copy of the memo "appears to have been written by Lieutenant Fox, but the final version was put out over Colonel Reeder's name, showing he agreed with the contents." In any case, the memo makes very clear the changes Fox wanted to see in the Twenty-Third's work:

> *The attitude of the Twenty-Third HQs towards their mission is lopsided. There is too much MILITARY . . . and not enough SHOWMANSHIP. The 603rd Engineer, on the other hand, contains too much ARTISTRY and not enough G.I. TACTICS. The successful practice of military deception by the Twenty-Third HQs requires the proper amount of both SHOWMANSHIP AND ARMY PROCEDURE.*

Fox noted past examples of the Twenty-Third's "failure to play its role thoroughly," and attributed the shortfalls to the unit's "servile obedience" to Army Regulations (ARs) and its "lack of appreciation of the fine art of the theater."

The first specific change Fox recommended was the need for shoulder patches and painted bumper markings that identified the unit that the Twenty-Third was replacing. He felt that such details were "just as much ammunition to a deception unit as 105mm shells are to the field artillery." There would be no excuse for not wearing patches for the unit they were replacing in the field. He recognized that painting bumper markings took more time than sewing on shoulder patches. Nonetheless, he believed that bumper markings were "equally essential to deceiving the locals, including any Nazi agents that might be among them."

Fox recognized that officers in regular units had no idea what the job of the Twenty-Third really was. He noted how a colonel scoffed at their work, believing "all you got to do is blow up the [fake] tanks and then you can go to sleep." Fox replied that the colonel "forgot that we were in show business." The dummies, he insisted "merely represent the 'scenery'—the PLAY must go on," as men "repair their tanks, hang out washing . . . and generally mill around in typical GI fashion." He reminded his men that no army equipment can function without gasoline, and so the trucks of the 603rd should make routine trips to the gas dumps and other supply depots.

Fox was adamant on another point: the presence of a general's jeep "with its scarlet license plate is essential," that is, a fake license plate. Although he knew that regular army brass would see that as contrary to ARs, he wondered, "Is not the whole idea of 'impersonation' [of another unit] contrary to ARs?"

Fox concluded his memo with three recommendations:

- The Twenty-Third should have an eye for details that would identify the unit they were replacing, such as road signs, sentry posts, and bumper markings.
- Men of the 603rd should accompany real officers whenever they could so the men could know the "tactical dispositions and the 'atmosphere' of fighting units."

- The troops should be familiar with the histories and orders of battle of the First Army, to get the "theater attitude" and be ready to impersonate any division or corps in France.

While Operation ELEPHANT was the Twenty-Third's first operation—and small at that, utilizing only about a third of its troops—the commanders learned a great deal that they would use in future operations. One critical thing they learned was that there needed to be closer coordination between the Twenty-Third and the other units. While the Twenty-Third knew its role in battle, "its needs, capabilities and limitations were completely unknown to the rest of the Army." Thus, the Twenty-Third took steps to correct that by establishing liaison officers to act as "DECEPTION 'salesmen'—selling and explaining deception to whomever would listen."

Another significant change in the operations of the Twenty-Third was a much stronger focus on what was called special effects, which included tactics to fool local, low-grade Nazi agents whose job it was to find out everything they could about the U.S. troops from observing shoulder patches and painted bumper markings and who were hoping to pick up information spread by GIs in shops and cafés. Using fake patches, markings, and other signage, as well as "accidentally" dropping false information for alert ears, would be a stronger part of the Twenty-Third's tactical repertoire. Special effects were even more important now because the Luftwaffe had been decimated earlier in the war and was almost completely absent from the skies over France, meaning that the value of the inflatable decoys in deception ops—despite all the work the men of the 603rd had put into designing and creating them—was greatly reduced.

A common thread in Fox's post-operation review and his memo is his insistence that the men must pay close attention to the details in an operation. Fox recognized that these little lies would add substance and realism to the big lie of each deception operation.

Following Operation ELEPHANT, the 3132nd Signal Service Company Special arrived in France. The entire Twenty-Third Headquarters Special Troops of artists, writers, and sonic experts would be available to assist the U.S. Army as it broke out of Normandy and fought its way across France.

Its next deception, Operation BRITTANY (August 9–12), was "mainly geographical." The Twenty-Third would be broken into four task forces that would move west on the Brittany peninsula while Patton's Third Army marched east toward Paris. The object of the operation was to convince the Nazis that the real American objective was to secure Brittany. In reality, Eisenhower wanted to trap the Nazis on the Brittany peninsula before they could escape and move east. The operation would be the "first time the Twenty-Third attempted to spread what was termed 'atmosphere' . . . the look and feel of a military unit in the area." In other words, the Twenty-Third was to put into operation many of the lessons it had learned about special effects after ELEPHANT.

BRITTANY called for four tank columns to simulate units of Patton's Third Army moving west. As Lieutenant Colonel Clifford Simenson put it, "We sent four columns out just to create confusion with no idea what we were doing. . . . It was the breakout of Normandy, and we just wanted the picture that Americans were all over the place." Fox used a football analogy to describe the situation as the Americans finally broke out of Normandy beaches. "It was a wild time—more like a kickoff situation," he wrote, "with players of both sides running all over the place. . . . Everyone, friend and foe, was confused."

Confusion notwithstanding, the Twenty-Third had its marching orders for BRITTANY, which would begin on August 9 and end three days later. The "story" of the operation was that the four units were moving west toward the port city of Brest, France, a Nazi stronghold. To reinforce the story, each column communicated through spoof radio messages with an advance party that was established on the Brittany peninsula.

Task Force MIKE simulated a combat team from the Thirty-Fifth Infantry Division with seventeen vehicles under the command of Lieutenant Colonel Mayo. MIKE actually made little progress and was only able to send and receive a handful of messages on their first day because the Germans were jamming their radio frequencies. As frustrating as that was for Mayo, he believed that even those few messages were enough to convince the Nazis that a column of real troops was moving west.

Captain Oscar M. Seale commanded Task Force NAN, which simulated the Eightieth Infantry Division on its way to Brest. Traveling at about 10 miles per hour, always on the lookout for Nazi snipers, they reached their bivouac area near the village of Pacé, a few miles from Rennes.

Seale dispatched about a third of his men to Pacé and nearby Saint-Gilles-du-Mené, letting locals know that the Eightieth Infantry Division would be arriving shortly. To complete the ruse, the following morning members of the 603rd, wearing fake shoulder patches and dressed as military policemen (MPs) from the Eightieth, were sent to Rennes to be seen by the locals. Things got a little too close for comfort when officers of the real Eightieth showed up at the bivouac area looking for their outfit. Locals had told them about the soldiers from the Eightieth that they had seen recently. The officers were "quietly told [by officers of the Twenty-Third] to forget everything they had seen and were pointed in the right direction."

For the next two evenings Captain Seale and Private First Class Charles Gorman dressed themselves as MPs of the Eightieth and went into Rennes, again to spread the word about the imminent arrival of the division. The fake MPs' favorite tactic was to go into local bars and loudly announce that it was now off-limits and the GIs in the bar should finish their drinks as soon as possible and leave. While the American GIs were finishing their drinks, Seale and Gorman chatted informally with many of the soldiers, spreading their misinformation.

Shortly after noon the next day, orders arrived to shut down the task force. The men of the Twenty-Third removed their fake patches and bumper markings and left the bivouac area a handful at a time in order not to call attention to themselves. Before long they were back in camp with the other members of the Twenty-Third.

The third task force was OBOE, led by Lieutenant Colonel Edgar W. Schroeder. On August 10, OBOE "transformed into a unit of the Ninetieth Division (put on patches, MP helmets, and removed bumper covers)" as the column moved from Le Mans to Rennes. The unit took sniper fire along the way, but their good luck held and they reached Rennes with no casualties. They were unable to make radio contact with the U.S. advance party at Lorient because the Germans continued to jam their frequencies. Nevertheless, the radiomen still transmitted situation reports of the unit's progress, just as a genuine unit would.

OBOE bivouacked on a hill overlooking Baud, where the men noticed German troops moving through a valley to the south of their position. Although there were scattered firefights between the Nazi patrols and bands of the French Forces of the Interior (FFI), the Twenty-Third did not engage the enemy. Their mission was to be a fake presence to help keep the Germans in Brittany.

The last of the task forces of the Twenty-Third was PETER, commanded by Colonel James Snee. PETER simulated three battalions (three hundred to eight hundred men each): a tank battalion, an armored infantry battalion, and an armored field artillery battalion. The unit left Sartilly early August 10 and bivouacked in an area a bit south of Martigné-Ferchaud. This task force was the only one involved in Operation BRITTANY that used inflatable decoys.

While the men of the 603rd spent their time setting up the decoys, others in the unit worked to create an atmosphere for the fakery of the Twenty-Third, telling tales in cafés and shops about the approaching convoy of U.S. soldiers. Still other soldiers drove the unit's trucks around the area, making sure that their phony bumper markings were obvious to any observers. That night the men of PETER noted with some satisfaction that a German plane flew near their bivouac area, a sign that the enemy was taking their presence as a credible threat.

Men of the 603rd were responsible for setting up fifty-four decoys, as well as thirty-two camouflage nets and nearly three dozen shelter halves (small tents for two soldiers). True to the decision the commanders of the Twenty-Third had made after ELEPHANT, locals were kept well back from the inflatable decoys.

The unit used a simple technique that showed how a good deception can be a force multiplier. Some of the men went swimming in a local stream, later moving on to another swimming spot. And another. All to give the impression that there were more U.S. soldiers in the area than were actually there.

At midnight on August 11, orders came for the men of PETER that it was time to pack up and quietly disappear. So, just as a stage crew will do at the end of a theater production, the men struck their set: deflating the decoys and packing them away, removing the fake shoulder patches, and scrubbing the bumper markings from the trucks and equipment. Following the practice of the other task forces, the troops left the area in small groups, heading back to the encampment, where the other members of the Twenty-Third awaited their return.

Was Operation BRITTANY a success? There is no conclusive proof that the Nazis altered their battle plans because of the deceptions of the Twenty-Third. However, as one World War II historian has pointed out, "Normally there is no one reason why things are done in war; decisions tend to be made for a number of reasons." There is general agreement, however, that the Germans thought the fake units in the area were real units. The enemy jamming of the radio frequencies is a good indication of that. The Signal

ARTISTS OF THE 603RD: ELLSWORTH KELLY

Ellsworth Kelly began his art training when he was eight or nine in New Jersey, when his grandmother introduced him to the joys of bird-watching by giving him a book on birds. Years later he recalled a little blackbird with red wings, which he said "seemed to be responsible for all of my paintings." Kelly "trained his eye to focus on shapes, forms, and colors, rather than lines." That's why many of his paintings "utilize only two or three colors, the same number that typically occur in any one species of bird." And it's that same limited palette that the artists of the 603rd utilized in their camouflage work.

Although his parents did not want to support his career in art, they allowed him to enroll in Pratt Institute in New York City, where they hoped he'd follow a more "practical" program in architecture or industrial design. He attended Pratt from 1941 to 1942 before he read a newspaper article about the camouflage work that the army was doing at Fort Meade, Maryland. He was immediately interested in being part of that unit.

He wrote to the army that he was an artist and was very interested in the 603rd. He was told that he had to enlist to be considered for the 603rd. Once he signed up, "we'll find you," the army assured him. However, the army didn't say *when* they would find him.

After Kelly enlisted, he spent a month in Fort Dix, New Jersey. When his transfer came through, Kelly was shocked to learn that he would not be traveling south to Fort Meade. Rather, he was heading nearly nineteen hundred miles west to Camp Cooper Hill, near Leadville, Colorado. Kelly's two months in Colorado helped him come to an important decision about his career as an artist. "I decided," he recalled, "that I didn't want to be a commercial artist. I wanted to be an artist just for me." Shortly after Kelly made that decision, he was transferred to Fort Meade, where he began working with the men of the 603rd. Among his assignments was to make posters for "training and morale purposes—to teach and inspire." In addition, he also worked with the other artists of the 603rd creating inflatable dummy tanks and trucks.

Once Kelly was discharged from the army, he studied at the School of the Museum of Fine Arts in Boston, from 1946 to 1947, before traveling to Paris. There, he studied with some of the most important artists of the time before returning to New York City in 1954.

Ellsworth Kelly received the 2012 National Medal of Arts from President Barack Obama, who called him a "careful observer of form, color, and the natural world" and "a vital influence in American art."

Company Special felt that the jamming was like the inflatable decoys being attacked by the Luftwaffe or taking artillery shells, a sure sign that the Germans had been fooled into thinking it was a real unit. The same could be said for the German reconnaissance flights in the area, indicating that the enemy believed that the Twenty-Third was a legitimate fighting unit.

In the larger picture, the work of the Twenty-Third in BRITTANY probably added to the confusion that the German commanders experienced. The Allies wanted to keep the Germans in Brittany and not give them the chance to retreat to the east toward Paris. The longer the Germans remained in Brittany, the greater the chance that the Allies could squeeze the Germans between Patton's Third Army in the north and the British and Canadian armies from the south. The Germans remained confused about what Patton might be up to. On the other hand, Patton had the advantage of intelligence he received from Allied intercepts, so he had a clearer picture of the confusion in the German High Command.

German confusion led to hesitation moving its army east. Consequently, one hundred thousand Nazi troops tried to escape through a narrow opening between the two large Allied armies that became known as the Falaise Gap, named for the small town in the middle of the pocket. The battle was fierce, leaving ten thousand German troops dead and fifty thousand prisoners. However, forty thousand troops managed to flee the gap, leaving behind most of their tanks, trucks, and artillery pieces. The retreat route was grim, "strewn with the dismembered bodies of horses and men, many of them grotesquely flattened by tanks." The Allies on the scene wore gas masks to keep out the reek of the corpses. It was what one historian called a "stunning slaughter and a great victory for the Allies."

If the operations of the Twenty-Third were minor and low-key to this point, that would change in Operation BREST (August 20–27), a mission that targeted the French port on the southern tip of the Brittany peninsula. Lieutenant Fox's assessment of the next operation for his men was clear and succinct. While the men showed "continued improvement in the technique of deception," he noted, there was also "a worsening in the employment of it." At this point in the war, Fox felt dissatisfied with the way the regular army utilized the deception techniques of his men. He continued to work for better communication between the Twenty-Third and the regular army.

Initially, the port was a crucial part of the Allies' strategy once they made their breakout from the Normandy beaches. The Allies thought Brest would be a vital port for supplies and equipment that would be shipped from England. However, with the success of the breakout, Patton's army made a sharp turn to the east toward Paris. Brest was too far out on the peninsula to serve as a supply port for an army that was already on its way into the heart of France. In addition, army commanders believed that the port would have been destroyed by the Nazis.

Even though the Allies didn't believe that the port of Brest would be usable, they wanted to silence the heavy coastal guns that covered the surrounding area and the approach from the sea so the Allies could safely bring in components for an artificial port they had planned for Quiberon Bay, about 120 miles southeast of Brest on the southern coast of the Brittany peninsula. As historian Philip Gerard put it, the operation was "simple and rather brazen: to simulate overwhelming armored force and thereby induce the German garrison at Brest to surrender."

The successful D-day invasion and the breakout from the beaches of Normandy had left the German army in disarray, its soldiers "giving up fairly readily," raising the hope that a show of force would demoralize the Nazi troops in Brest, who might surrender if faced by a significant force. It was up to the Twenty-Third to pretend to be that "significant force." At the same time, the Allies were concerned about the German paratroopers at Brest, under the command of General Bernard Ramcke. He had sent some troops out on a daring raid to rescue their men captured by the French Resistance, and the Allies were worried that they might repeat the raid to threaten their supply lines.

What the men of the Twenty-Third didn't know was that Allied intelligence had grossly underestimated the number of German troops at Brest. Rather than facing twenty-one thousand Nazi soldiers who might be quick to surrender, the U.S. Army faced thirty-eight thousand seasoned paratroopers who were not about to give up without a fight. General Ramcke would see to that.

A portion of the Twenty-Third, under the command of Colonel Snee, left its encampment in Le Fremondre on August 20 and traveled 190 miles to its bivouac area near Lesneven on the following night. At that point, the unit was divided into three task forces, called X, Y, and Z. Each headed to a different site to carry out its deception mission.

Task Force X was commanded by Captain Oscar Seale and included four platoons of camouflage engineers, a sonic platoon, and a platoon of engineers. Around midnight, the engineers set up fifty-three tank decoys. The deception plan called for one company of tanks—from the 709th Tank Battalion, to add some real tanks to the scene—to look like the entire Fifteenth Tank Battalion. The real Fifteenth had moved off a few days earlier.

Setting up the decoy tanks that night was a challenge for the men of the 603rd. Some of the dummies would not hold air because of leaky valves. The weather dealt the men another challenge: pouring rain. After hours of work, the men had "only leaky pup tents with muddy floors to go back to for a few hours' rest before daylight."

The sonic boys cranked up their heaters, the huge speakers on the back of the sonic half-tracks, so the German troops could hear the tank battalion arriving. At the start, they played their "music" for thirty-minute intervals, with five minutes of silence between each program. Later they added ten-minute periods of silence, with each "show" simulating fifteen to twenty medium tanks lumbering into position and then harboring for the night.

This combination of decoys, spoof radio, special effects, and sonic deception was "superb," according to Lieutenant Fox. While the deception may have been skillfully executed, the operation had tragic consequences for the real tank battalion. Because of a lack of communication between the 709th Tank Battalion and the Twenty-Third—one historian speculated that perhaps they did not know the Twenty-Third even existed—the tanks and their support marched into "what was, in effect, an American-induced ambush."

The Germans, hearing the fake tanks of the Twenty-Third and seeing the decoys, believed that an armored division was approaching Brest. They countered what they considered an imminent attack by setting up a huge force of anti-tank guns and artillery along the main road leading to the city. The 709th "blithely and naively decided to attack down the road where the Germans were expecting Patton's armor. It was an unmitigated disaster."

Four tanks were destroyed before they had gone very far; another was incapacitated. In addition, two tank commanders were killed and two crewmen critically wounded. To make matters worse for the 709th, Company Two lost four more tanks the next day, leaving three more tankers dead. Artist Ellsworth Kelly had bitter memories of the debacle. "The real tanks retreated through us," he remembered, "and their crews were screaming at us that we should have joined them—'If you had been with us, we wouldn't have had to retreat! You let us down!'" Corporal Bill Enderlein, a member of the Twenty-Third who rose to the rank of colonel before he retired from the army, came upon the devastation suffered by the 709th and was sick at heart. "When I saw all the carnage," he recalled, "I said, 'Did we cause this?' It was horrible."

While Task Force X and Z were to simulate tank units, Task Force Y, under the command of Lieutenant Colonel Mayo, included two platoons of *camoufleurs* from the 603rd squad of combat engineers to provide security, and a wire team. The overall mission of the fifty-four men in Task Force Y was to use flash devices to simulate the muzzle flashes of 105mm howitzers in a way that diverted enemy attention from the Thirty-Seventh Field Artillery Battalion. The Thirty-Seventh needed protection to conduct its mission of supporting an attack on Brest by three U.S. infantry divisions without coming under fire themselves.

Task Force Y used no inflatable decoys, just a maze of wires to set off the flash devices about a thousand yards from the real guns of the Thirty-Seventh. The men of the Twenty-Third knew they could expect to attract counter-battery fire from German artillery. So when the men were told to dig their foxholes deep, they did just that, fearful of the deadly shrapnel from German shells that would fly through the air as they drew fire from German artillery. Their operation was, the men of the Twenty-Third realized, "absurd, potentially suicidal." One of the soldiers in the Twenty-Third, Sergeant Jim Laubheimer, mused long after the mission, "How we came through it, I'll never know—I really don't. Sometimes we did stuff that was absolutely stupid."

The four loaders in each team of five men slid a flash bomb containing a cup of black powder into a tube that was made from a used 90mm antiaircraft shell casing, which had a diameter of 3½ inches and was nearly two feet long. When the charge of powder slid home, the men ducked into their trench as they awaited the flash that mimicked one from a 155mm field gun. The black powder was set off by an electrical charge that flowed from a large battery through a wire similar to the heating element in a toaster. The wire, glowing hot, would ignite the flash. The team waited. Five seconds. Ten seconds. "Suddenly the flash shot out of the tube in a brilliant flare of sparks with blinding surprise." The firing didn't always go according to plan, especially when the powder was damp or the batteries had run down and couldn't supply enough of a current to heat the wire.

The flash devices were set up about three-quarters of a mile ahead of the real guns of the Thirty-Seventh Artillery Battery. Telephone communication was established with the Thirty-Seventh's Fire Direction Center to coordinate the flashes with the occasional real firing of the guns to the rear. After all, muzzle flashes, no matter how realistic, would not fool the Germans without the thunder of real guns.

The whole point of the operation was to fool the German artillery to fire at the wrong target and allow the real U.S. artillery to fire at the enemy positions, protecting the troops that would be assaulting Brest. To add realism to the ruse, radiomen filled the air with spoof transmissions, becoming the "least visible and in certain ways the most effective" component of the operation.

Task Force Z, commanded by Lieutenant Colonel Cliff Simenson, set up its array of a dozen decoy medium tanks and six decoy light tanks among a handful of real tanks. The dark and continuous rain made the job difficult. When ready, the inflatables were put into the usual strategic position for tanks, facing the enemy, providing them less of a target than the side of a silhouetted tank. In addition, a tank facing the enemy was ready to fire its deadly turret gun and move out quickly if necessary. Such an arrangement of the tanks also allowed the *camoufleurs* to conceal the decoys' wheels, which would not pass a close inspection.

While some members of the task forces were setting up inflatable decoys and their flash artillery devices, others were taking up the Twenty-Third's recent emphasis on special effects. Simenson ordered some of his men in Task Force Z to show more activity around the decoy sites, something more theatrical. He ordered his men to set up more pup tents, fire up smoky stoves for cooking meals, and hang out their clean laundry. A tank from the Sixty-Ninth drove around the area, covering the ground in strategic places with tank tracks.

In addition, their trucks, marked with the insignia of the Sixth Armored Division, cruised the roads of the nearby village for all the locals to see. While there were two soldiers in the cab of the truck, the Twenty-Third's added touch had two men sitting close to the tailgate of the covered back of the truck, facing each other, giving the impression to any spies watching the U.S. trucks that each was filled with soldiers.

At one point, Captain Thomas C. Perry of the 709th joined Simenson in an inspection of the work of the Twenty-Third. The men observed the simulated tank arrangement through binoculars from a church steeple at Milizac. They were both pleased with what they saw. Perry reported that he couldn't tell the difference between the fake tanks and the real ones arranged along the road so troops and locals would easily see them.

Once again, however, miscommunication between the Twenty-Third and the army nearly caused another calamity. Lieutenant Colonel Simenson gave the order for his sonic unit to be in position to begin playing their sound effects between 10:45 and 11:45 p.m. However, none of the officers of Task Force Z knew that the real attack was to begin at 11:00 p.m. Lieutenant Colonel Snee of the Twenty-Third found out about the imminent attack by accident when he wandered into the staging area for the troops. He was furious over yet another example of poor communication between the Twenty-Third and the regular army. As he wrote in his report, had the sonic equipment started at 10:45, it might have stirred the Germans to strike fifteen minutes before the infantry attack. Had that happened, the assault troops could have walked into another deadly ambush of enemy artillery.

Despite the command errors that resulted in tragedy in one instance and a near repeat calamity in another, the theatrical performances of the Twenty-Third were well reviewed. One observer for the Second Infantry Division found the sonic program especially convincing. He appreciated the details of the deception, such as "the normal intervals between tanks for night driving, normal rate of speed, intervals between companies," as well as "shifting of gears, tread noises, crackling of brush and voices of guides" giving directions to tankers. An assistant operations officer of the same unit noted that the "sound effects throughout the entire operation were extremely realistic" with "no distortion."

Was Operation BREST a success? Once again, assessing the success of a deception operation falls into a murky area. The easy answer is no. After all, the Nazis at Brest were not intimidated by the action of the Twenty-Third to give up and surrender without a fight. In fact, Ramcke's men stubbornly held their ground for nearly three weeks after the Twenty-Third closed down its operations, which was longer than expected, costing ten thousand American casualties.

However, there are mitigating circumstances that affected the assault of Brest. For one thing, U.S. general Troy Middleton was encouraged by the higher command to move slowly in his attack on Brest in an attempt to minimize U.S. casualties. In addition, U.S. intelligence had woefully underestimated the makeup and the number of troops under Ramcke's command. Rather than commanding a garrison of ordinary soldiers, the German general had a "very dedicated and professional force of soldiers." The terrain around the walled city had been groomed for defensive purposes over many years, which made it difficult to expel the German forces from Brest.

In the big picture of the work of the Twenty-Third, their three early operations in France—ELEPHANT, BRITTANY, and BREST—gave the officers and enlisted men the chance to hone their skills. They learned from each operation, gaining a better understanding of how their skills and expertise could best help the fighting army beat the Nazis.

After Operation BREST, the Twenty-Third packed up its decoys, flash devices, and other assorted tools of deception and moved east, deeper into France.

CHAPTER 5

THE FIRST BIG TEST

While the Twenty-Third was engaged in Operation BRITTANY and Operation BREST, General George Patton was driving his Third Army east across France. Ten weeks of bloody battles since the D-day landing at Normandy had taken a heavy toll on Allied soldiers. While General Bernard Montgomery, commander of the British Twenty-First Army Group, and General Omar Bradley, commander of the U.S. Twelfth Army Group, pushed Allied Supreme Commander General Dwight Eisenhower to permit them to make direct attacks into Germany, Eisenhower preferred a slower, more methodical approach that allowed the Allies to conquer all the retreating and surrendering Germans—hundreds of thousands had been captured—and to secure the liberated territory in France.

As the U.S. Army marched east, they liberated towns and

This Allied assault on Arnhem, a city on the Dutch-German border, unsuccessfully attempted to end the war with a massive airborne attack. Eisenhower later wondered if had he not attacked Arnhem, "possibly we could have begun the Walcheren attack some two or three weeks earlier."

The Allies could not wait for Antwerp to be secured. They desperately needed supplies. To make matters worse, much of the rail system in France had been destroyed by Allied bombs, so it could not serve the Allies as a means of moving supplies to the troops. To replace the use of rail, the Allies organized the Red Ball Express, a massive operation of trucks that drove around the clock to move supplies to the troops.

In the meantime, the Allies took a breather to reorganize and take stock of their troops and supplies. While the Allied soldiers no doubt welcomed the break, it was also good news for the bedraggled and nearly beaten German army. The lull gave the Nazis time to regroup and retreat behind the fortifications of the Siegfried Line. They refused to throw down their weapons in the face of the Allied onslaught. Instead, they stood their ground and fought back with a surprising ferocity.

Unfortunately, American military leaders underestimated the formidable problem that the Siegfried Line would pose. The Siegfried Line, which originated in World War I, was a defensive line of forts, pillboxes, and tank defenses that stretched nearly four hundred miles from Kleve in the north, near the Dutch border—along the German border with Belgium, Luxembourg, and France—to the boundary of Switzerland in the south, and included more than eighteen thousand bunkers and dragon's teeth, which "consisted of

THE RED BALL EXPRESS

The Allied troops racing across France from Normandy—more than 250,000 soldiers and support personnel—needed *lots* of supplies. General Omar Bradley wrote in his autobiography that each of the twenty-eight Allied divisions that advanced through France and Belgium "ordinarily required 700–750 tons [of supplies] a day—a total daily consumption of about 20,000 tons." In addition, such a force requires plenty of gasoline. In fact, Patton's Third Army and General Courtney Hodges's First Army used a combined total of eight hundred thousand gallons of gas on an average day.

The Red Ball Express took its name from railroad slang for an express train. The two-phase operation started on August 25, 1944, and ended eighty-three days later, on November 16. The first phase lasted until September 5, but necessity demanded that the program be extended.

The plan called for the "exclusive use of a one-way loop highway, operating round the clock and utilizing all available motor transport." Initially, the highway ran from Saint-Lô to Chartres. Later the highway was extended east to Paris, and then even farther east to Metz and the Belgian border.

The first problem facing the Red Ball Express was finding enough trucks. The U.S. Army had 132 truck companies in France, but it needed 240 to keep its express going around the

An MP (military policeman) in front of a
tote board marking how much cargo had
been moved by Red Ball Express drivers

clock. So the army began "borrowing" trucks from all sorts of
units: "evacuation hospitals, gas treatment battalions, mobile
refrigerator companies, salvage and repair companies, engineer camouflage units, signal depot and repair companies,
ordnance maintenance companies," and more.

The next problem was finding enough drivers for the
trucks. When the army began looking for drivers, "African
American troops, in large measure, kept the supply lines rolling." In fact, 75 percent of the Red Ball Express drivers were
African American and "the majority of the quartermaster truck
companies . . . were manned by blacks."

Drivers were expected to follow certain rules of the road to
maximize the time spent moving supplies. To ensure that the
trucks maintained a constant speed, governors were installed
on the engines to restrict the speed on each truck to 25 miles
per hour. It didn't take the drivers and mechanics long to

remove the governors to allow the trucks to cruise at 60 miles per hour. The drivers were to keep sixty yards between vehicles and were allowed a ten-minute break ten minutes before every even hour. One historian noted that, despite the rules for the drivers, the Red Ball Express was "more like a free-for-all at a stock car race."

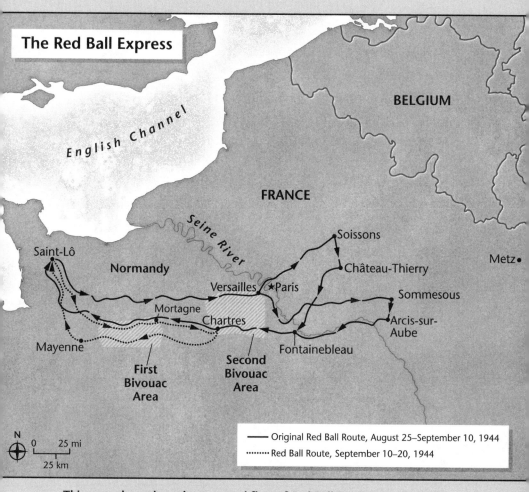

The Red Ball Express

This map shows how the eastward flow of Red Ball Express trucks took the northern leg of the loop while the returning trucks traveled along the southern leg. The map also shows the two bivouac areas that serviced the drivers and trucks on both legs of the trip.

The pace and schedule of the Red Ball Express took its toll on the vehicles and the drivers. Tires were shredded from driving over roads littered with shell fragments, barbed wire, and other battlefield debris. For the drivers, the most dangerous part of their work was night driving. One veteran of the Express recalled, "I've driven when I couldn't hardly see, just by instinct. You sort of *feel* the road." Another Red Ball driver remembered "falling asleep on top of a jeep hood when it was raining like hell. I didn't know the difference."

Despite all the hardships on men and machines, the Red Ball Express played a critical role when U.S. troops desperately needed supplies. By the time the operation ended, "more than six thousand trucks and trailers and some twenty-three thousand men transported 412,193 tons of supplies." In a memo to the officers and men of the Red Ball Express, Eisenhower declared that the "Red Ball Line is the lifeline between combat and supply." Although it was largely an on-the-fly operation, the Red Ball Express "contributed significantly to the defeat of the German Army in France."

truncated pyramids of reinforced concrete standing in rows on a single concrete foundation, each one three to four feet tall," with foundations sunk a yard or so deep. Such obstacles were designed to slow down enemy tanks and funnel them into a narrow kill zone, a common defensive strategy. The fortifications were built in several phases, starting in 1938 and ending two years later. Each phase featured various structures, beginning with small pillboxes with twenty-inch-thick concrete walls and three forward-facing openings through which the Germans could fire at the enemy. The bunkers in the next phase of construction were larger and stronger, with cement ceilings and walls that were five feet thick and large enough to accommodate up to a dozen soldiers.

With the Allies stretched along the Siegfried Line, the Allied commanders were certain that the Germans would offer little resistance. For the Allied troops, "home by Christmas of 1944 became a possible dream." That dream was shattered when the Germans offered a stout defense of their fatherland.

Things worsened for the Allies when Operation MARKET GARDEN, the brainchild of General Montgomery, utterly failed. Designed to get around the Siegfried Line and secure critical bridges over the French river Moselle, the operation had two parts. MARKET called for American paratroopers from the 101st Airborne to land and capture key bridges at the northern end of the Line. GARDEN was to be a ground attack up Highway 69 in which Allied troops would connect with the paratroopers in three or four days. In the event that any of the bridges had been blown up by the Germans, an engineering unit and bridging equipment would be part of GARDEN.

armored unit. (The real Sixth was beginning to make its march east from Lorient, France, about five hundred miles away.) The fear among the Allies was that the Germans would realize how weak that gap in the line was and punch through to attack Patton's left flank. Filling that gap with its fakery would be "the riskiest ploy [the Twenty-Third] had yet dared."

The men of the Twenty-Third were to utilize four means of deception: spoof radio, sonic effects, inflatable tank decoys, and the increasingly important special effects. The unit was divided into three main groups.

- The Twenty-Third Headquarters Company would simulate the divisional headquarters of the (notional) Sixth Armored Division, while men of the 406th Engineers would play the role of MPs attached to that unit.

A decoy Sherman tank

- Combat Command A (CCA), led by Lieutenant Colonel Schroeder, would include a company and a half from the 603rd, a group of signalmen, and a platoon from the 406th.
- Combat Command Reserve (CCR) would have a makeup similar to CCA and would be commanded by Captain Seale.

The men of the 3132nd sonic unit would remain near the divisional headquarters until it was time for them to play their role in Operation BETTEMBOURG.

The men of the Twenty-Third set to work, each doing his part to make the deception a success. Some began creating an "atmosphere" that would show anyone watching that the Sixth Armored Division had arrived. Special effects received priority from some men who sewed on appropriate shoulder patches. There weren't enough patches for everyone in the notional division, but it was not uncommon that some soldiers did not wear the patch of their unit. Other men painted the Sixth's insignia on the bumpers of the half-tracks, jeeps, and trucks. When their handiwork was finished, they drove around the countryside, making their presence known in surrounding villages. Captain Rebh's combat engineers established phony checkpoints to direct the fake trucks that were arriving. Truckloads of American soldiers visited villages, to be seen in cafés, bars, and even in local churches.

Because the eight thousand men in the imaginary army would need a lot of water, for themselves as well as for their vehicles, engineers built a phony water point in plain view of the locals in Bettembourg. Platoons of men arrived three times a day to fill jerry cans with water.

Lieutenant Colonel Simenson noted that "civilians were observed photographing bumpers, taking notes, and asking 'friendly questions'"—which was fine with Simenson, who wanted that false information to get back to the Germans. Getting such misinformation to the enemy was, after all, exactly the point of creating an "'atmosphere'—the observable, convincing evidence of a buildup."

The inflatable tank dummies were not a major part of BETTEMBOURG. Only about half of the two dozen brought by the Twenty-Third were used, and they were only inflated at the start of the operation. The decoys were supported by a platoon of real light tanks that were part of the Forty-Third Cavalry Squadron, which was in the area. The reason for using a limited number of decoys was a familiar one. There was very little aerial reconnaissance at that point in the war that might spot and report the phony tanks. Sometimes, the tank dummies, which were often set up in the dark, needed to be turned around at first light so they were all facing in the right direction.

A more compelling reason to curtail the use of dummies was that the area in which the Twenty-Third was operating was so close to the German border that the Americans felt there was a real danger German agents and their sympathizers could discover that the tanks were fake, bringing down the whole deception operation. To add realism to these fake tanks, five genuine light tanks played their part, moving along country roads so the locals could spot them. Nevertheless, if the Germans realized what the Twenty-Third was doing and counterattacked, they would easily plow through any resistance from a band of *camoufleurs,* sound-effects men, and radio platoons guarded by a handful of combat engineers.

The men of the Twenty-Third were not shy about pretending. In fact, Lieutenant Fox, with his background in drama at college, "loved this part of the war—playacting in minor farces and dramas." The small groups of his men that drove from one local village to another were "like advance men for a traveling show, drumming up business in town while the main troupe was setting up out at the fairground."

Fox took a special delight in "barreling through the neighboring towns; displaying our Armored insignia and two-star license plate; guarded fore and aft by jeeps bristling with machine guns." The men with fingers on the triggers of the .30 caliber machine guns "scouted the high windows of nearby buildings where snipers usually hid."

While the machine guns were real, the officer riding in the jeep with the red, two-starred license plate of an American major general was a fake. As Fox wrote, "Nothing gives the sense of Importance better than High Ranking Brass." In this case, that role was played by a "middle-aged Princeton alumnus with a military moustache." Fox himself was happy to play the fake general's aide-de-camp.

On one such trip near their new base in Luxembourg, the "major general" and his motorcade stopped at a bar that was owned by a Nazi sympathizer. The general and a few of his men barged into the bar, where he barked an order. His men disappeared into the storeroom and emerged in a few minutes carrying six cases of wine, some of the best that the owner had to offer his customers. He scowled at the Americans, but he knew it was useless to protest.

The Americans didn't need the wine. In fact, Fox "despised looters in any army." But he knew that their actions were arrogant enough that the owner couldn't help but report the looting to the Nazis. That the theft of the wine was led by a major general of the Sixth Armored Division would no doubt confound the Nazis. The Sixth in Luxembourg? Abwehr, the German intelligence agency, placed that division in Brittany. This misinformation would work its way up the German command ladder and perhaps alter their order of battle to the advantage of the Allies, by moving some of the troops that were defending Metz.

Since spoof radio would be an important part of the overall deception, the Signal Company Special began laying sixty miles of wire for field telephones between the Forty-Third Cavalry Squadron and XX Corps Headquarters. The Twenty-Third would not use radio transmissions for real communication with headquarters but rather for transmitting misinformation, knowing that the Germans would intercept such transmissions and, the Twenty-Third hoped, make flawed battlefield decisions based on the phony information in their intercepts.

The men of the Signal Company Special knew that their work involved more than simply sending a lot of fake messages. In fact, sending too many messages could easily unmask a deception operation. They needed to pay attention to the number and timing of their radio messages. A good signalman "can tell a lot about what a unit is doing just by watching the number of radio transmissions, even if he cannot understand what is being said." The Signal Company Special determined that an operation of the size and type being mounted by the Twenty-Third would normally require about seventy messages to be sent during its course. Consequently, the signalmen held their radio transmissions to that figure.

In addition to special effects, another area that improved since the unit's initial operations in France was the cooperation between the Twenty-Third and the regular army. Neither wanted a repeat of the tragic consequences of poor communication of the earlier operations. XX Corps allowed the Twenty-Third's signalmen to use already established radio networks, furthering the illusion that the fake transmissions were from an established unit and not one new to the front.

In order for BETTEMBOURG to be a true force multiplier—one of the objectives of the operation—it needed to give the illusion that the small band of deceivers—about 750 enlisted men and officers—was a much larger armored division. One of the methods to create this deception was to manipulate the traffic of trucks and troops in the operation.

A crucial part of any large troop movement was the Main Supply Route (MSR). A division's MSR was a critical route that needed to be well marked and patrolled. In a true army operation, the MSR kept the troops and supplies moving. In a fake operation like BETTEMBOURG, the MSR gave any local Nazi agents and sympathizers false information to pass on to their handlers. And, like other aspects of a deception, the movement of military traffic needed to be realistic.

To complete the deceptive MSR, road signs were painted and posted along the notional MSR. These signs included code names for the Sixth Armored Division (BAMBOO) as well as the location of command posts for Combat Command A (BACON) and Combat Command Reserve (BACK). Fake MPs, played by Captain Rebh's combat engineers, patrolled the MSR and were stationed at key intersections and crossroads to direct any stray vehicles. In short, everything that a real army division did when it moved to a new location was very carefully mimicked. All for the benefit of any of those ground agents that Simenson's men noticed taking notes about the movement of U.S. troops and equipment.

Another ruse used as a force multiplier was the old trick of driving a small number of trucks through towns multiple times, changing the bumper markings after each trip. So a truck that drove through a town with the markings of an artillery division, for instance, returned later in the day with the markings of an infantry division. Two soldiers again sat at the back of the covered trucks, giving the appearance that the vehicles were filled with men.

Because of the proximity to the German troops on the other side of the Moselle, an important component of BETTEMBOURG was the work of the sonic players. After Seale's CCR unit arrived at its bivouac area late one night, two officers from the 3132nd sonic company made a quick reconnoiter of the area. At three a.m., the rest of the unit arrived and began setting up shop. Within an hour, their sonic program was blaring tank sounds from their heaters across the river.

The 3132nd was to simulate three notional tank battalions. Since that meant about 160 tanks, the sonic program needed to be varied and convincing. As in other operations, the sonic show began with the sounds of tanks moving into position, then harboring in place. The programs ran for twenty minutes, followed by a ten-minute break. The roar of the powerful engines, the clanking of the transmissions, and the clatter of the treads were all part of the sonic show of the 3132nd. According to reports, "the sonic deception was considered very effective." Vic Dowd, with the 603rd, noted that the "enormous sounds of tracks racing through the forest sounded like a whole division was amassing." The heaters were blaring. He remembers that the sound barrage included a sergeant yelling at one of his men to "put out that goddamned cigarette now." Dowd also remembers being told that the Germans were "jumping on anything they can find to get the hell out of Luxembourg."

As the operation dragged on, the sonic unit made sure their programs were loud and clear as they boomed and crashed into the darkness for four nights. Fox later heard from an army G-2 (intelligence) officer that the Nazis nick-named the Twenty-Third's Sixth Armored Division the "Phantom Division," indicating a unit that seemed to be everywhere yet couldn't really be seen. "That made us feel good," Fox later wrote. The men of the 3132nd appeared to be doing their job convincing German ears that nearly 160 tanks were amassed on the other side of the river, itching for action.

But it wasn't only the Nazis that were hearing the sounds coming from the heaters of the sonic unit. Lieutenant Dick Syracuse of the XXX Corps recalled how his eyes were "beginning to tell me what my ears were hearing. Psychologically it was the most unnerving thing. I would actually begin to see tanks in the dark." The work of the 3132nd sonic unit was *that* good.

Despite the success of all aspects of Operation BETTEMBOURG, it took its toll on the men of the Twenty-Third. For one thing, the weather turned brutally cold with a

ARTISTS OF THE 603RD: VICTOR DOWD

Like many of the creative young people who were members of the 603rd, Victor Dowd knew from an early age that he was going to be an artist. He recalled that his mother "never had to worry about me on rainy days, because I'd occupy myself by drawing." A "soft-spoken kid with a subtle and quick sense of humor," Dowd was the class artist in elementary school.

He attended Pratt Institute, where he heard an appeal from an army general who told the senior class that the army was looking for artists. The general's words stayed with him, although following graduation he joined other young artists drawing superhero comics for a New York studio that created the likes of Bulletman, Captain Battle, Doc Savage, and the Shadow. In fact, two of the artists at the comic-book studio—Ray Harford and Bob Boyajian—joined him when he signed up for the army. It was not a tough decision for Dowd, since, in his Brooklyn neighborhood, "everybody was in the service."

It's no surprise that Dowd started his artistic career by drawing comic books. By studying the illustrations in popular magazines, Dowd "marveled at the lines, the color, how a stroke here or there could create a mood, a facial expression, a sense of movement." He became quite adept at drawing people, a talent that he honed while he was in Europe with the Twenty-Third.

Dowd arrived in France on June 14, 1944, and he was immediately face-to-face with the horrors of war. As soon as the new soldiers marched off the transport plane, twenty-four stretchers with badly wounded men—those who had "lost arms and legs, who had been ripped apart by artillery fire and were held together by bandages" and worse—were loaded on the plane, which quickly headed back across the English Channel. He was "struck by the wild difference between last night [in England], when I was in the lovely, quiet, serene countryside, and the grim reality of today."

Before the Twenty-Third reached its new home base in Luxembourg, Dowd was among the men who spent time in Paris, recently liberated by the American army. He was surprised how his sketchbook acted as an invitation for people to talk to him, many asking for him to draw their portrait. Like the other artists of the 603rd, he was happy for the chance to practice his craft.

Fortunately, Dowd had experiences that were a relief from the horrors of war. Years after the war, he still remembered the French woman who saw him sketching in Briey and invited him home for dinner with her family. The woman asked if he would sketch her daughter. The GI was glad to oblige. He planned to return the next day to finish the sketch, but "there was no next day—we moved out. And I felt bad about that." However, the story had a happy ending when Dowd's mother, who was French, brought the sketch with her on a postwar trip home to France. She made a side visit to Briey and asked if the postmaster recognized the girl in the sketch. It turned out that the girl was his granddaughter! Finally, the woman who had extended a kindness to Dowd received the sketch of her daughter.

For his service under fire before the Americans could break

out of Normandy, Dowd was awarded the Bronze Star. After the war, Dowd became a commercial artist, continuing his work on comic books before turning to advertising, working on ad campaigns for large corporations such as Pepsi and General Motors. Before he retired, he illustrated twenty books and spent fifteen years as a fashion illustrator.

steady rain. As Jim Laubheimer wrote to his family, "By this time, we had also learned to wear all of our extra clothing, so it was not unusual to have two sets of long underwear covered by two pairs of . . . trousers and two wool shirts. . . . Add a field jacket, raincoat, a wool hat under a helmet, and gloves . . . and one can see that we looked like fat teddy bears waddling about the woods!" In the bivouac area, the men were not allowed to have fires yet, so they "joined their shelter halves to make large tarpaulins for shared dryness and warmth."

But the physical hardship the men of the Twenty-Third endured during the week of Operation BETTEMBOURG was only part of the tension they had to deal with. They also had to face the stress of an operation that many men of the unit sensed had gone on too long and could take a deadly turn for the worse at any time. Technician Fifth Grade E. Gordon Wilson Jr. recalled after the war that he could never understand why the radiomen were placed so close to several large guns. "Every time a gun fired," he wrote, "our whole unit bounced and rocked from the concussion."

On September 17, two days after the Twenty-Third had established its bivouac area, the Germans became more active along the front. They moved an infantry division (at least ten thousand troops) near a division already in place. Nazi patrols were spotted a few miles south of the Twenty-Third's position. The men were used to German patrols coming close to their position, but these were mainly small-scale moves to test the lines. On occasion, U.S. soldiers engaged in firefights with German patrols. One such patrol penetrated to within two thousand yards of the sonic half-tracks. Although the Americans did not engage in any major action with the Germans, orders were given to prepare for an evacuation of the position if a major German attack materialized.

The men of the Twenty-Third were tense. Some of them "strung tripwires attached to tin cans around their bivouac areas" as a warning of any German intrusion. The men expected calamity, knowing that they did not have the firepower or troops to stop a major German attack. Even Colonel Reeder, the commander of the Twenty-Third at headquarters more than two hundred miles away, was more nervous with each passing hour of the deception. He and his officers understood that they were pushing their incredibly good luck by extending the ruse beyond a couple of days. Too many things could go wrong and doom the operation, putting U.S. lives at risk. Even small things, like a careless conversation by Americans in a café, could be overheard and reported by one of the many Nazi collaborators. While BETTEMBOURG had gone nearly flawlessly, the pressure to maintain that level of success "ratcheted up the anxiety level."

But the German breakthrough that all had dreaded as the days dragged on never happened. Instead, the men of the Twenty-Third received news that none of them expected. Not only had the Germans withdrawn from the area, but they had blown up their own bridge at Remich, in Luxembourg. The Nazi troops had retreated across the Moselle. They would no longer be able to attack with their fearsome armored divisions. It was time for the Twenty-Third to pack up and leave.

Operation BETTEMBOURG was by far the Twenty-Third's longest deception of the war, but was it a success? Lieutenant Colonel Simenson thought so, remarking that only with

Operation BETTEMBOURG "did things come together and the unit begin to operate as it should." He described it as "our first operation that was executed fully professionally and correctly." So the operation was well executed, but was it successful? It seems to have been a practical success, in that it drew more substantial German patrols into the Twenty-Third's area. And, more important to the Americans, two German divisions from Metz were moved there, reducing the defenders of that walled fortification.

By the end of September 25, all the members of the Twenty-Third were together again, this time in Luxembourg City. Lieutenant Fox wrote that "even the most pessimistic did not predict" that the capital of Luxembourg would be the headquarters of the Twenty-Third until the following spring. The men settled in, the staff in the large German and Italian foreign ministry buildings. The headquarters company and the 3132nd sonic unit were billeted in a school, while the engineers and Signal Company Special took over a big seminary, "full of atrocious Nazi murals." As Fox described them in a letter to his wife, "Usually, they are either glorified, sentimentalized or cute pictures of soldiers at war. One barracks . . . had a playful Nazi hanging his laundry on a line strung between the horns of two smiling giraffes. . . . The Nazis have such a tendency toward bad taste." Nevertheless, with the entire unit finding accommodations more comfortable than their pup tents on the hard ground, Fox noted that "It began to look like the Twenty-Third was bedding down for the winter."

About ten days after the Twenty-Third returned to their new quarters in Luxembourg City, they were on the move again. The new operation reflected a change in the front, as it had shifted north through Luxembourg into Belgium. Operation WILTZ (October 4–10, 1944) would be much less complicated than BETTEMBOURG, as it was created to cover the movement of the Fifth Armored Division from an area near Fels, Luxembourg, to Malmédy, Belgium, about sixty miles north. The objective of the deception was to make the Germans think that the Fifth was staying where it was.

The original plan was ill conceived. How could the commanders think they could move a division of tanks—between 250 and 300 tanks—sixty miles during the day and imagine that none of the locals would notice what Fox called "the huge, clanking columns [that] blocked the road in full daylight"? The alternative was to move the tank columns at night. But that plan required the tanks to "black out," or remove all visual means of identification. It turned out to be impossible to pull off that sort of deception maneuver on such short notice.

Realizing that the movement of the tanks out of the area near Fels could not be concealed or disguised, the Twenty-Third decided to "ride with the punch" and concede that the Fifth had moved but attempt to convince the Nazis that the tank division had not gone as far north as it actually had.

The new deception plan called for one fake combat command (CCA) to stop in the vicinity of Malcheid, Belgium, about twenty miles south of the real CCA's location. A second combat command (CCB) settled near Wiltz, Luxembourg, about thirty-five miles south of the real Fifth. The emphasis for both deception units was spoof radio, and as one historian noted, the signal aspect of the endeavor would turn out to be "a large step forward" for the signal unit.

The signal unit used seventeen radios over an area of

A real tank (left) next to a decoy tank

one thousand square miles. One of the reasons the signal deception was so successful was the fact that the radiomen of the Twenty-Third began "infiltrating" the real radio networks two days before the actual operation was to begin. The extra time gave the radio operators of the Signal Company Special the luxury "to be briefed thoroughly by the real Fifth Armored operators and gradually take over the operation of the nets." Fox thought the transition from genuine Fifth Armored radio transmission to the fakery of the Twenty-Third was seamless and the enemy radio intelligence would have had a hard time detecting it. The radio operators of the Twenty-Third used the Fifth's call signs, frequencies, cipher system, and distinctive traits, or the "fist" of each genuine operator.

Of course, for the spoof radio operators to fool the Nazis, the real Fifth had to maintain radio silence for the duration of the operation. In the meantime, to convince the Germans of their location, the spoof operators sent occasional radio checks but very few actual messages. However, when "real" messages were sent, each one "fit perfectly with the situation that was being portrayed." As in other spoof radio operations, the radio operators of the Twenty-Third were careful to not simply fill the airwaves with fake messages that could alert the enemy to the deception.

In addition to spoof radio, the Twenty-Third wore shoulder patches of the Fifth Armored Division. However, since there were not enough patches for all 650 men in the operation, about half of the patches used were painted by the 603rd Special Effects Section. From a distance or in a moving vehicle, the painted patches would appear authentic to any Nazi sympathizer.

Other special effects were utilized in WILTZ. For instance, the notional Fifth visited the water point with the same regularity of trips that men of the genuine Fifth made before they moved out. Nine light and medium tanks were part of the deception, to add "atmosphere" to the operation and to cover the ground with the telltale tread marks of an armored division. It was such attention to detail that had become the hallmark of the Twenty-Third's operations.

Simenson's CCA settled near Walscheid, France, to give the Germans the impression that that was as far as the Fifth had traveled. The Twenty-Third was to mimic an armored infantry unit as well as a headquarters unit. The CCA chose a heavily wooded area for their bivouac and arranged the vehicles in the unit around the edge of the woods to give the impression that more troops and vehicles were hidden there. To complete the bivouac scene, the Twenty-Third again used special effects. Campfires were lit, directional signs were posted, and MPs guarded the perimeter of the area.

Another special effect was to stencil bogus unit markings on the bumpers of the vehicles. Technician Fifth Grade Wilson explained that the equipment and trucks had no such markings on them when they left base in Luxembourg City. When they arrived near the bivouac, they drove into a secluded wooded area, where the team responsible for identification gave some of the men Fifth Armored shoulder patches to sew on their uniforms. While the men were sewing on their patches, another team stenciled the Fifth Armored identification on the front and rear of the equipment. As Wilson recalled, "When we left the woods we were an entirely different unit."

Some of the special effects the Twenty-Third used in WILTZ were similar to the ones the men used in earlier operations, like having some of the troops visit towns and be seen in cafés and shops. Volunteers attended church services on Sunday. Other men drove about the countryside with shoulder patches and vehicle bumper markings obvious. A new special effects stunt was sending two fake MPs to a local police station to report that one of the Fifth's vehicles was missing. If they found it, would the police see that it was returned to the (notional) Fifth camp?

The men of the 3132nd weren't left completely out of the operation. They did blast some tank sounds one evening from seven thirty until nine o'clock. Mixed in with the tank sounds was the noise of men moving bridge-building material into place. The sonic men added the sounds one would expect to hear around a camp, like officers barking orders to enlisted men, troops shouting to their buddies, laughter.

Toward the end of WILTZ, the tanks in CCA, bivouacked near Walscheid, changed places with their counterparts in CCB, near Wiltz, in an effort to give the Germans the impression that more tanks were arriving at both sites. All the while, the real Fifth Armored Division was at Malmédy, Belgium, awaiting its orders.

On the evening of October 8, the troops in the Twenty-Third were allowed to listen to game five of the World Series on the radio, between two teams from the same city. The Saint Louis Cardinals won a pitchers' duel against the Saint Louis Browns, 2–0, the only runs in the game scoring on two home runs.

At midnight October 8, Operation WILTZ was terminated. One by one, radios were shut down. The following day, the men began their departure from the bivouac areas, after markings of the Fifth Armored Division were removed from vehicles and the division arm patches were removed from uniform shirts. The men of the Twenty-Third left the area in small groups at fifteen-minute intervals, heading south to their home base in Luxembourg City.

Was Operation WILTZ a success? Not in a tactical sense since the Fifth Armored Division never saw action at that point in the war. So there's no way of knowing if the Germans were fooled by the operation. Due to the unconcealed movement of the Fifth Armored Division, Fox felt that the chance for success of WILTZ was "greatly endangered." As far as Fox was concerned, the "big lesson re-learned . . . was the absolute necessity for coordinating deceptive efforts with the actions of the covered unit." It was an issue that continued to plague the Twenty-Third.

While Lieutenant Colonel Schroeder was looking at the strategic success of an overall operation, the men of the Twenty-Third performed admirably as they needed to adjust their strategy when it became apparent that the initial plan for moving the Fifth had no chance of working. Fox believed that the radio operation went smoothly. He felt that the efforts of the Nazi operators to break into the spoof radio nets was an indication of some degree of accomplishment, "as satisfying to the Signal Company as the shelling of rubber dummies was to the Camouflage Engineers. And not as scary."

The big takeaway from WILTZ for Fox was how the Twenty-Third and the genuine army again realized the critical necessity for coordinating deception efforts with the actions of the units the Twenty-Third was covering. Fox understood that the success of his radio operators was directly linked to the two days they spent "infiltrating" the radio nets of the Fifth Armored Division and learning from their radio operators.

While most of the troops returned to Luxembourg, a sonic task force headed north for what was planned to be their first foray into Germany. However, that operation, dubbed VASELINE, never materialized. Once again an effort in conjunction with the Fifth Armored Division, VASELINE figured to be "loud, short and possibly furious" because the area was under heavy bombardment from Nazi artillery. The operation was to last only one night, just long enough to give the Fifth the chance to surprise the Germans with an attack from a position farther south. After several postponements, VASELINE was cancelled, as the Fifth was deployed in another area. The sonic team returned to join their unit, where, as Fox put it, the men "mostly enjoyed Luxembourg" for the next three weeks.

5/44

CHAPTER 6

A TRIO OF DECEPTIONS

When the soldiers of the Twenty-Third arrived in Luxembourg in late September 1944, the country had been recently liberated from Nazi control. In time, the men would be "overwhelmed with affection for the people of Luxembourg, who opened their homes to them and struck up friendships that lasted for decades." One woman explained why she welcomed American GIs: "I wanted to give them the thing they yearned for most—a warm friendship and the 'home' they have missed for so long." Another woman said at a gathering of American troops, "Four years of bitter sorrow and restless daily fight have vanished in that one moment we saw the first of you smiling boys."

Even with the warm reception the troops received from many of the people of Luxembourg, they still had work to do, and in early November 1944, the Twenty-Third was again called to the battlefield. This time they were to be divided into three units, to participate at the same time in three separate operations at different places along the front. Named DALLAS, ELSENBORN, and CASANOVA, these simultaneous operations "stretched the abilities of the Twenty-Third to the limit."

Operation DALLAS (November 2–10) was designed to help the American siege of Metz, which had festered since the end of September. The members of the Twenty-Third involved in this operation were tasked with establishing a fake artillery presence near Jarny, France, a short distance from Metz. The operation would allow the XX Corps artillery to move north to a new position, where the big guns could support an assault of Metz by the Ninetieth Infantry Division, an attack that would lead the way for Patton's Third Army to push on to the Rhine River.

The operation was under the command of Lieutenant Colonel Mayo, the Twenty-Third's artillery officer. His unit consisted of 195 men with thirty-six dummy artillery pieces, along with camouflage nets and flash simulators, integral parts of any fake artillery operation. Although special effects would also play a part in the deception, there would be no spoof radio or sonic shows in DALLAS.

The nearly two hundred men of the Twenty-Third that set to work in Jarny were not enough to take the place of the 2,230 men and forty-eight pieces of artillery in the XX Corps artillery, which had moved out under cover of darkness. But in keeping with the recent order for genuine units to cooperate with the Twenty-Third, XX Corps provided five hundred troops and a dozen "real shooting pieces," which gave the operation a more realistic look. For this deception,

A dummy artillery piece

the Twenty-Third again stenciled division markings on the vehicle bumpers as soon as they arrived. In addition, they sewed on their notional shoulder patches.

At dusk on November 3, the men inflated the tank decoys and set them up under the camo nets. However, they encountered a problem with some of the nets. They were starting to rot after having been kept too long in a damp storage area. The days and nights of cold rain only made the problem worse. Nevertheless, the decoys and the real artillery pieces were moved into place.

As in other deceptions, great pains were taken to make sure that the normal routine of the departing unit was maintained. So fires were lit at the gun locations to help the gun crews fight off the cold and rain. The fires didn't seem to do much good, however. Bob Tompkins wrote in his diary: "Squads alternate firing [the flash devices] and guard every day. Rain, wind, and mud make for a horrible existence. Our hut is leaking like a sieve. Everything is soaked. Don't see how an attack can start in this weather." The following day, he continued, offering more insight into the daily life of a member of the deception team: "Spent horrible night on guard. . . . Soaked to skin. Is pouring again. . . . Can plainly hear machine gun fire, mortar and rifle fire about a mile away. Artillery shakes the hut."

The fake artillery followed the same pattern in its firing sequence as the departing unit. The real guns were fired between the reports of the flash devices, making it more difficult for the Nazis to know how many guns were firing. Not all that many volleys were fired during the November 2–10 operation—perhaps one hundred rounds, about the amount one would expect from an artillery unit in a quiet sector.

Guard posts were established around the perimeter of the firing area to keep out curious locals or those looking for intelligence to pass along to the Nazis. To maintain the integrity of the inflatable guns, each had "one man with it at all times [during the day] to make sure the dummy gun maintained air pressure." However, the guard was useless in dealing with the wind that pushed around the fake large guns. The crew attached sandbags to the fakes, as well as tied them down. Nevertheless, the problem persisted. Some of the fake artillery pieces' barrels wrinkled and caved in, a problem that was solved by "packing mud on the inside to push it out to a normal shape."

Even though nearly all the men and big guns of the XX Corps had departed, the Corps' observation airplanes maintained their scheduled flights over the area. On November 8, a German spotter plane circled the unit which, of course, the Twenty-Third took as a sign that the Germans believed that real artillery pieces were still in the area.

With the big guns of the XX Corps in place near Metz, the operation was shut down on November 10. The men of the Twenty-Third cleaned all the fake unit markings from their vehicles and removed their fake shoulder patches. Then, in small groups, they left the area in ten-minute intervals and headed back to their home base in Luxembourg City.

The evaluation of the operation was typically vague about whether the mission could be termed a success. No one could say for sure. But the operation's leaders did say that they needed more men for future operations like DALLAS. They felt it would benefit an operation if the engineers didn't need to work with the inflatables, fire the flash simulators, *and* pull guard duty.

When the artists of the 603rd returned to their billet and had some free time, they welcomed the opportunity to grab their art supplies and wander the streets of Luxembourg City, stopping to paint a scene or sketch a captivating face. Private Ned Harris carried his supplies in a German grenade case. Harris also stored his finished drawings in the case. As he noted, the grenade case was "a receptacle for death, and I was bringing these lively drawings to fill it up."

Like many men in war, the artists of the 603rd cherished their free time when they were not on an operation. Not that they had a lot of it. There was plenty to keep them busy at the home base in Luxembourg City. As Hal Laynor wrote to his wife, "I had to laugh when you ask me what time we work, we can work from six in the morning to six the next morning." The men spent those work hours checking and repairing equipment or driving around in a jeep or a two-and-a-half-ton truck on a special effects assignment. They could pull guard duty of their billet or deliver supplies to other units in another part of the city.

One constant for the men, no matter where they were billeted—north side of Luxembourg City for the main force or south side for the sonic unit—was the cold, nasty weather. Their uniforms did little to keep out the chill and the rain. Consequently, most of the men in the unit wrote home asking for heavier clothing: sweaters, gloves, thick socks, and scarves. The men "scrounged or built stoves for every billet, even dugouts in the field. Fox carried a stove in his jeep."

Most of the unit lived in a school building. And even though it lacked some of the amenities of stateside barracks, the artists were grateful that they had a dry place to store their paintings and sketches and safely leave work that they planned to complete at another time. The artists appreciated that they could buy or barter for art supplies they needed, like good heavy paper stock, new pens, and tubes of paint.

Hal Laynor was giddy in a letter to his wife, telling her that he was "art conscious again & I've painted three paintings that are almost up to my old standard in watercolor. . . . I'm trying to make at least two or three paintings a week now."

The men of the Twenty-Third also had the good fortune to enjoy a visit from glamorous film star and singer Marlene Dietrich. "Bundled up in a shapeless wool suit," the exotic

Dietrich sang a few of her famous songs in "the only live USO show ever to visit the Special Troops." Hal Laynor acted as master of ceremonies for the show and did some stand-up comedy. Laynor also made sketches of the star so he could paint her later.

While Operation DALLAS involved only a bit of special effects and no spoof radio, Operation ELSENBORN (November 3–12), under the command of Lieutenant Colonel Schroeder, featured only those deception tactics. This operation involved thirty-six officers and 431 enlisted men, about a third of the entire unit. Because spoof radio would be such an important part of this operation, nearly half of the enlisted men (193) were from the Twenty-Third's Signal Company Special.

For this operation, the setting would be like nothing the Twenty-Third had encountered before. Rather than work in the field near the front line, this operation was to take place in and around Camp Elsenborn in Belgium, an army camp between Eupen and Malmédy, close to the front lines. ELSENBORN "revolved around a complicated series of division moves," which had the Twenty-Third simulating the Fourth Infantry Division at the rest camp, when in reality the Fourth was heading north for a deadly confrontation with the German army in Hürtgen Forest. The forest became a "deathtrap . . . [where] the Germans wiped out whole units of American soldiers with tree bursts, artillery shells fused to explode in the treetops and shower thousands of lethal splinters into troops caught in the open." When the fighting ended in Hürtgen Forest, the Fourth suffered more than seven thousand casualties.

One of the signalmen in the Twenty-Third, E. Gordon

ARTISTS OF THE 603RD: ARTHUR SINGER

Arthur Singer was another member of the 603rd who started his craft at an early age. Although he went on to earn an international reputation as a painter of birds, his first subjects were the neighborhood cats. Raised in New York City in a family of artists, Singer made frequent family outings to the Bronx Zoo, where he began to draw lions, tigers, and other large cats. He also visited the American Museum of Natural History, where he continued to develop his skill.

After high school, Singer attended Cooper Union, a highly regarded college specializing in art, architecture, and engineering. In 1943, after graduating from college, Singer worked as a printer and in an advertising agency for a few years before joining the army, where he conceived camouflage schemes for tanks, which "required keen observation of terrain and moving objects when viewed from the air."

After serving in the army, Singer found his niche as an artist of birds. His first major assignment was to create eleven pages of color illustrations for the bird section of an encyclopedia, work that "established him as a modern Audubon," the legendary nineteenth-century painter of birds. Singer's artistic career took off in the early 1960s with the publication of the definitive study *Birds of the World,* for which he painted all the illustrations, solidifying his reputation "in the first rank of the world's finest bird artists."

Self-portrait by Arthur Singer

The list of books in which his art appears is long and wide-ranging, including *Birds of North America, Birds of Europe,* and *Birds of the West Indies.* However, Singer's most popular work didn't appear in a book. In 1982, the U.S. Postal Service asked him to create a series of postage stamps, "Birds and Flowers of the 50 States," with his son, Alan, painting the state flowers. The series sold more than 500 million sets of fifty stamps and "is believed to have been the largest-selling special issue in the history of United States postage."

Before his death in 1990, Arthur Singer won a number of awards for his work, including a lifetime achievement award from Cooper Union and the Audubon Society's Hal Borland Award.

Wilson Jr., had clear memories of the seventy-five mile drive from Luxembourg City to Elsenborn. As the unit neared their destination, their route took the convoy along an open road near the crest of a ridge. He remembered thinking that the front was somewhere out there. Perhaps as close as two miles. Wilson was "enjoying the drive and the beautiful valley spread out below" when he spotted a "small plane" flying over the ridge from the east, heading west. As he watched the plane, its engine cut out and then it turned north and hit the trees on a nearby hill with "a tremendous explosion that spread fire all across the top of the hill for probably a quarter of a mile." The spectacle was his introduction to the Nazi V-1 rockets that had been the scourge of London.

Before the unit reached the camp, the task force stopped at a wooded area and each man was handed a shoulder patch for the Fourth Infantry Division. This is where Wilson and the rest learned which unit they would be mimicking for the next few days.

When the men of the Twenty-Third arrived at Elsenborn, Wilson couldn't help but wonder, as the V-1s roared overhead, how reliable they were. The V-1 flights became unnerving for the men, as during the day, "one would fly over every ten minutes—everyone would hesitate—listen to make sure it would make it—then get back to what they were doing." Night flights of the V-1s screamed overhead every twenty minutes. Fox recalled how the rockets "made the windows shake. And sometimes they seemed to sputter and stall."

Since the Twenty-Third's early operations had all been conducted in the field, working at a rest camp presented a new set of considerations. The most obvious one was that the men of the Twenty-Third had no idea what a division did in an enclosed area for rest and recreation. They dealt with that issue by sending a team to see what the men of the Ninth Division did when they were at the Elsenborn barracks. The recon team took "careful notes . . . on such things as signage, distribution of military policemen, local patrols, and water distribution points."

A bigger problem that needed careful deliberation was the fact that a unit's radios were normally silent when that unit was at an R & R camp like Elsenborn. This meant that the Twenty-Third would have to abandon one of its most

A radio operator in action in the field

valuable tools or else come up with a reason for radios to transmit while in the rest camp.

The commanders of the Twenty-Third decided they needed to execute "a fake within a fake." Working with the Ninth, the Twenty-Third would establish a pattern of daily radio tests that would continue when the notional Fourth arrived. No doubt the radiomen of the Ninth were more than a bit upset when they got the news that part of their "rest" time at Elsenborn would include a daily test of the radio sets and their operators. But this ruse would be the key to fooling the Nazis about the whereabouts of the Fourth Infantry Division.

While part of the Twenty-Third was working with the Ninth to establish daily radio tests, signal experts from the unit were sent to the Fourth bivouac area near Bullange, Belgium, to study their transmissions and operators, learning the idiosyncrasies of the radiomen they were going to imitate. Ten radio teams arrived to take notes on the operators. The Twenty-Third received complete cooperation from the men of the Fourth, who understood that a successful deception operation could save soldiers' lives. As the signalmen of the Twenty-Third learned the quirks and habits of their counterparts in the Fourth, they slowly took over sending messages for the Fourth while they were still at Bullange. By November 5, the radios of the Fourth were operated only by the men of the Twenty-Third, setting the patterns of what they would do in Elsenborn to convince the Nazis that they were actually intercepting transmissions sent by the Fourth.

On November 6, the signalmen of the Twenty-Third, posing as their counterparts in the Fourth, received orders to observe radio silence as the division moved to Elsenborn, a standard practice when a division was on the move. They set up their radios at the R & R camp and began sending the prepared practice messages that were included in orders sent to the radiomen. The script contained a list of sixteen messages like these:

- Patrols third Bn [battalion] have taken seven enemy prisoners.
- Activity slight. Baker and Charlie reported nothing and Able reported only slight patrol action. Dog Company had some trouble in their sector but OK now.

World War II historian Jonathan Gawne believes that in addition to these practice messages, a German agent might have heard "some grumbling from signalmen who had to give up some of their free time to take part in some ridiculous radio test."

The entire operation used twenty-two radios dispersed around the camp as the Ninth had distributed their radios. The radios were worked by one hundred operators. Major Charles Yokum, the Twenty-Third's signal officer, was very pleased with the operation, recommending it be used as a model for future operations, not only for other Twenty-Third radio spoofs but for the other units that the Twenty-Third worked with. He remarked that the "time allowed for planning and coordinating, the cooperation given by all headquarters involved, were the best encountered so far"—a dramatic improvement over the Twenty-Third's earlier operations. The spoof radio part of the operation went smoothly, but officers realized that one of the main reasons the deception was successful was because the unit was in a confined area of the camp. This operation did not have the men or vehicles to pull off such a deception in an open area.

While the signalmen of the Twenty-Third were pretending to be the radio operators of the Fourth Infantry Division, other members of the unit went into action with special effects. Or as Fox put it, "The rest of the play was filled out by artists from our Special Effects Section," acknowledging that his men were working together in their high-stakes make-believe.

On November 6, vehicles with covered bumper markings drove to the command post of the Fourth. The genuine Fourth moved out to the north to an assembly point near the Hürtgen Forest. At that point, off came the bumper covers and off came the raincoats that had hidden the Fourth shoulder patches, and the Twenty-Third became the Fourth Infantry Division, heading for rest and recreation at Elsenborn barracks.

With the trucks on their way to the rest camp, the Special Effects Section had more work to do in the field to complete the ruse. Fake MPs were assigned to key road junctions to direct the vehicles to the camp. Near the camp, signs were painted with markings indicating the way to the divisional command post, where the medical battalion should go, and so forth. And since no troop movement of that nature was complete without MPs, phony MP positions were maintained day and night in nearby towns to direct traffic (and help spread misinformation).

At the camp itself, the Twenty-Third did its best to follow the patterns established by the Ninth Division, the previous occupants of Elsenborn. Jeeps manned by MPs delivered food. Water points were used with a frequency that indicated they were serving an infantry division of at least ten thousand troops. Vehicle patterns of the Ninth were also maintained. Messenger vehicles, wire patrols, mail trucks, and trash trucks made the rounds as they had normally been made.

Technician Fifth Grade Wilson scoffed at the idea of a "rest camp," which he felt "was definitely not our idea of resting. In order to look like a division of ten thousand men in rest camp our small group [of about 430 enlisted men] had to do a lot of things that I would not call resting." He went on to say that his unit had to "keep . . . moving around in the area so any local inhabitants would see action and report it to the German friends. . . . On all of our operations we had to consider that any civilian could be a spy/informer for the German Army."

On November 11 at six p.m., orders were received that Operation ELSENBORN would end the following day and the Ninth would return to the camp. Under cover of darkness, the bumper markings were washed off and shoulder patches removed. The unmarked vehicles of the Twenty-Third began leaving Elsenborn barracks at three-minute intervals.

With the unit back in Luxembourg City, Richard Morton and Walter Arnett of the 603rd continued creating their cartoons. However, it didn't take long before the men got into hot water with army brass for their work. They'd hung their art on a bulletin board in the barracks. Officers who were ridiculed in the cartoons found nothing amusing in them. Colonel Otis Fitz and Major William D. Hooper issued a memo prohibiting cartoons and announcing stiff penalties for violation of their "standing order": six months of hard labor and forfeiture of two-thirds of their pay for that period. Before the unit cartoonists could feel the wrath of the order from Fitz and Hooper, General Eisenhower had the good sense to issue an order of his own overriding the prohibition of cartoons.

The final of the three deception operations was CASANOVA, which can be called a classic deception operation . . . that never happened. The idea was to showcase "all the tricks in the Special Troops inventory" except the dummies, which were in the field in DALLAS. In fact, CASANOVA was to be such a "must-see" demonstration that officers from the French and Dutch military were on hand to observe the Twenty-Third in action.

Operation CASANOVA was more complicated than DALLAS, involving the sonic unit in support of an attempt by Patton's army to cross the Moselle into Germany. As the general had said, "Throughout history, wars had been lost by not crossing rivers." And Patton was eager to cross the Moselle and take the war to the Germans on their own soil. The main deception of the Twenty-Third was to use the sonic skills of the 3132nd to "create all the clatter and commotion of a major bridging assault" at Uckange, France, while the Ninetieth Infantry Division, with support from the Tenth Armored Division, crossed the Moselle about a dozen miles downstream near Thionville. The objective of the deception was to draw German troops away from Thionville to Uckange.

The detachment of the Twenty-Third that was to be CASANOVA was under the command of Lieutenant Colonel Simenson. Smaller than the DALLAS detachment, it included fifteen officers, 265 enlisted men, and sixty-four vehicles, forty-two of which were from the sonic company. But the special effects men were to do their usual work of making an infantry battalion of four hundred to one thousand troops look like a division of ten thousand men. They would drive and walk around the area near Uckange, making their presence known to any lurking agents. And, as usual, they also marked the bumpers of vehicles, put up road and directional signs, and assigned fake MPs to strategic crossroads.

Meanwhile, the sonic trucks of the 3132nd set up shop on the banks of the Moselle. They were ready with their bridge-building "clatter and commotion," which included recordings of the roar of large construction equipment, men shouting orders, and steel modules of a Bailey bridge being slammed into position. All they needed was the order from Simenson to launch their show.

At the last minute, Major General H. L. Twaddle, commander of the Ninety-Fifth Infantry Division, which was actually going to cross the Moselle downstream, changed his mind and decided that he and his troops would cross the river at Uckange. Twaddle decided he did not want the sonic deception of the Twenty-Third calling attention to the spot where his division would cross the river. His engineers began work on a bridge across the Moselle, the "longest Bailey bridge in the world," according to one historian. So the 3132nd was out of business. The Special Effects Section "merely splattered the . . . area with Ninetieth Division atmosphere."

As it turned out, the crossing was a stunning success for the U.S. forces. Taken completely by surprise by the attack of the Ninetieth Infantry, the German army suffered a

》》》

BAILEY BRIDGES

One key strategy of warfare is the destruction of bridges by a retreating army to stymie a pursuing army. Before World War II, there was no fast way to rebuild a destroyed bridge until the British set about to find a solution to that battlefield problem. Early in World War II, armies had relied on the pontoon bridge, but these bridges generally could not handle thirty-five-ton tanks, rolling heavy artillery, and large equipment trucks.

Donald Bailey of Britain's Royal Engineers designed a portable bridge in 1940 that came to bear his name. His engineering marvel was easily transported and could be assembled in a short amount of time with basic tools and a relatively small group of soldiers. The Bailey bridge was a huge success. By the end of the war, General Dwight D. Eisenhower, Supreme Allied Commander, said that, along with radar and the heavy bomber, the Bailey bridge was "one of the three pieces of equipment that most contributed to our victory" in Europe. British Field Marshal Montgomery said he "could never have maintained the speed and tempo of forward movement [in Italy and Northwest Europe] without large supplies of Bailey bridging."

Early in the war, the American army was so impressed with the design and strength of the Bailey bridge that it requested construction drawings from the U.K. In the summer of 1941, the U.S. Army received full design drawings of the bridge and began exploring the modifications that it would need to make

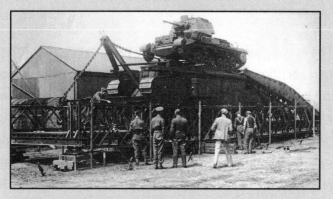

A Bailey bridge under construction

in the design, like changing the nuts and bolts from millimeters to inches, so it could begin production of its own version. After much trial and error, the U.S. Army began deploying its version of the Bailey bridge. It's been estimated that by the end of 1943, American factories were building an average of two Bailey bridges a day, building up "the vast store of them" that would be required for the landing on D-day.

The Bailey bridge proved very popular with General Patton's Third Army. One engineering battalion supporting Patton's army was the 488th, which consisted of about six hundred men. They built forty-one Bailey bridges, totaling 4,812 feet. And because the Twenty-Third worked in tandem with the Third Army, the noise of bridge construction was one of the sound effects recorded and played by the sonic unit of the Twenty-Third.

Part of what made the Bailey bridge such a success in the war was that pieces of the bridge could be easily transported. No special equipment, such as cranes, was necessary to assemble a Bailey. Parts fit on a regulation army three-ton truck, and a small convoy could move all the parts needed to build a bridge. Small crews could "throw these bridges across streams and gullies in a few hours."

CHAPTER 7

A DEADLY WINTER

In the month after CASANOVA, the inactivity of the Twenty-Third "led to boredom, obesity," and bickering among the men as they were "kept busy and unhappy taking basic courses in military courtesy, interior guard, first aid and sanitation." To make matters worse, the weather was getting colder by the hour. However, the boredom of life at the home base ended when the Twenty-Third received orders to move out for another mission. They would once again have the chance to do what they were trained to do. But, as it turned out, the members of the Twenty-Third nearly got more than they had bargained for.

Their next operation, KOBLENZ (December 6–15, 1944), was a week-long deception aimed at an eighty-mile stretch in a fairly quiet section of the Allied front lines. The area in which the operation was staged was near Luxembourg City, what Fox called "the dullest part of the Western Front." The area was held lightly by the VIII Corps and used mostly as a rest area for weary divisions or as a training area for newly arrived divisions.

On the other side of the Moselle River, the German soldiers were encamped in an area that was similar in purpose. If the Twenty-Third could convince the Germans that KOBLENZ was a legitimate troop buildup of the Seventy-Fifth Infantry Division, it would accomplish a couple of objectives. First of all, it would hold the German troops in place and make them unavailable to move to the north when the Americans decided to attack there. Second, were the Germans to be duped by the deception of the Twenty-Third, they might even bring in reinforcements from the area around Metz, to the south, leaving that area more vulnerable to U.S. assault. And since the area across the Moselle was where the Nazis gave new troops "a short course of leisurely combat" before shipping them out north or south on the front lines, KOBLENZ might also keep the Germans from training such green troops and force them to use these new outfits to defend against an assault that would never happen.

The "story" for the deception was that a U.S. infantry division was gathering its forces in preparation for an attack on Koblenz, Germany, after a march up the Moselle valley. The identity of the notional division to be used in the deception changed four times in the few weeks leading up to the start of KOBLENZ, until the Seventy-Fifth Infantry Division was finally chosen because its recruits had recently arrived from England and the deception planners felt that German intelligence would not yet have a good fix on its location.

The objectives of Operation KOBLENZ, according to the

"story" of the deception, were "to split the German forces on [the German] side of the Rhine River and . . . to capture the rocket launching sites in the vicinity of Trier." The deception called for the operation to be postponed a number of times to keep the Nazi army fixed in place as long as possible. KOBLENZ would be eventually canceled, keeping the Nazis from knowing that the operation was really a ruse.

One of the big differences between KOBLENZ and earlier deceptions of the Twenty-Third was that, as Fox wrote, his unit "did not handle it all by ourselves. Our Deception Team acted in a supervisory capacity for VIII Corps and, of course, supplied most of the deception players and devices." On November 15, the Twelfth Army Group ordered the Twenty-Third to create a deception plan that would keep the German troops on alert in the VIII Corps region.

The VIII Corps' chief of staff insisted that all personnel cooperate with the deception plan and the men of the Twenty-Third. More than that, the commander of VIII Corps, General Troy Middleton, was very concerned about the security of the operation. He allowed KOBLENZ to move forward only after rigorous counterintelligence measures were established. He insisted that the number of personnel who knew the operation was a deception be as small as possible. Middleton also requested that the Twenty-Third maintain "proper counterintelligence measures, and safeguards" to make sure that no information about the operation or the involvement of the Twenty-Third leaked to the enemy.

On December 9, the U.S. Army Air Corps began bombing sorties over the area, a typical tactic to soften up the attack zone before troops move in. Other measures were taken to show signs that an attack was imminent. Artillery batteries moved into position and then set up some decoy 155mm field guns. In addition, reconnaissance patrols began moving deeper into enemy territory, as if searching for weak spots in the German defenses.

As in past operations, the Twenty-Third's vehicles arrived in a large wooded transit area, this time near Arlon, Belgium, to prepare for their move into action. Patches for the Seventy-Fifth Infantry Division were given to about 40 percent of the men who would be in the most visible positions. All the men carried sewing kits, so they were ready to attach their shoulder patches.

While some of the men worked on their unit patches, the trucks of the Twenty-Third received their usual makeover. The paint-and-stencil crews painted the Seventy-Fifth division insignia and other false identifying marks on the front and rear bumpers. The work on uniforms and vehicles complete, the unit appeared "to be a completely different organization from the one that left Luxembourg that morning."

When men and machines of the deception unit reached their new positions, they were given their assignments. Some of the soldiers were sent out on continuous reconnaissance missions, "usually in the middle of driving snowstorms, keeping an eye on the German lines through binoculars. They wanted no surprises."

Wilson and another technician fifth grade were given a map of the area with orders to drive their truck along certain roads, but to return over different roads. Of course, such maneuvers were common for the Twenty-Third, part of the usual strategy to make the locals believe that the U.S. Army presence was greater than it actually was, creating a force multiplier. It was hoped that two hours of driving back and forth would fool the enemy into believing that all the vehicular activity was part of the U.S. buildup.

When Wilson and his driving partner finished their shift behind the wheel, they turned their map and truck over to another team for their two hours of doing the same thing. When not on the road, Wilson observed that the radio operators in the unit were involved in a number of activities: "operating a radio, doing guard duty or other duties, sleeping, eating or just plain resting when they found the time." And, of course, the artists in the unit were always quick to take out their pencils and paints and capture what they saw in their sketchbooks.

The men of the Twenty-Third, veterans of eight other deceptions, had learned what they needed to take with them in their trucks when they left their home billet in Luxembourg City for a mission. In addition to the usual—clothes, toiletries, and, for many of them, their art supplies—they had their "10-in-1" boxes of food. As Wilson remembered it, "10 meals for 1 man or 1 meal for 10 men . . . and each truck was always supplied with two or more of these boxes." Actually, each box offered meals for ten soldiers: breakfast, a midday snack, and an evening meal. The food for breakfast and lunch was packed together for group cooking and was "similar to the offerings in the K-rations: various canned meats and stews, butter spread, powdered coffee, pudding, jam, evaporated milk, vegetables, biscuits, cereal, beverages, candy, salt, and sugar, as well as the typical accessories of cigarettes, matches, can opener, toilet paper, soap, towels, etc." The dinner was essentially a snack, with "only biscuits, candy, sugar, and gum, and was separately packaged (small tin cans in boxes . . .) so it could be easily handed out to

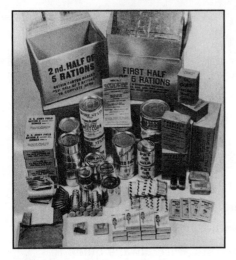
10-in-1 ration boxes

soldiers who were on the move during the day."

There was plenty of work for the men of the Twenty-Third to do to get the Germans to believe that the eleven hundred soldiers of their unit were really a division of more than ten thousand getting ready to attack. In addition to the fake truck traffic, the men set up large supply areas, partly hidden by a poor job of camouflage, just enough for the Germans "to think we did a sorry job of hiding things that we wanted to hide." They used the same shoddy camouflage practice to almost hide the simulated fuel dumps as well as dummy tanks and other large equipment with camo nets.

The 603rd used a wide array of rubber decoys for fake guns, tanks, and small observation planes, all tied down to keep them from blowing out of place. In addition to the dummies, the 3132nd ran its sonic program with the sounds of heavy vehicles "that could be heard over a mile or more away and would convince you that you heard all those tanks, guns and [pieces of] equipment actually moving." Each day for eight days and nights, there was an increase in sonic activity and noise. While the sonic unit was cranking out sound, the half-tracks drove in between the tank decoys, making a maze of tracks, giving any observer the impression that a lot of tanks had been through the area.

As usual with deception operations, security of the area was of paramount importance. Anyone not a member of the operation was not allowed near any of the deception equipment. The guards made sure "no outsider could get close and at a distance it looked and sounded like the real thing."

There were other jobs that needed to get done by the Twenty-Third to "sell" the idea of a growing number of U.S. soldiers and fire power. Men erected signs, directing vehicles to the command post and visitor parking, and giving traffic directions. Men were sent out on bogus road patrols and convoys, while others visited local towns to spread misinformation. The bumper markings and shoulder patches clearly advertised that the Seventy-Fifth Infantry Division had arrived in force.

The fake 275th Engineer Company performed "the visible duties of a real divisional engineer battalion," such as maintaining the water point, trucking coal and gravel, and making minor road repairs. The heavy equipment of the 406th was "particularly helpful in creating the picture of a division engineer unit."

Another significant part of KOBLENZ was the work of the Signal Company Special. It simulated five radio networks, the traffic-control chain network decidedly the most active. Using a code system that the Americans were sure the Germans could break, messages were sent along a six-point "chain" of radio transmissions that allowed the Nazis to follow the progress of the notional Seventy-Fifth Infantry Division along its eighty-five-mile west-to-east route from Sedan, France, to Sandweiler, Luxembourg, near Luxembourg City. As the fake troops marched on to the deception area, the sonic unit played additional sounds of columns moving, creating the impression that many more vehicles than had been seen during the day were arriving.

One German prisoner of war, who believed he had been captured by the Seventy-Fifth, scoffed at army radio operators, accusing them of being "very sloppy in their radio traffic." He went on to brag how the Germans had easily broken the code used to send U.S. radio transmissions. It appeared to U.S. intelligence that the Germans never considered the possibility that all of the "traffic chatter" they intercepted could have been part of a U.S. ruse.

At about 11:30 p.m. on December 15, the Twenty-Third received orders to pack up and return to its home base. The drive home after KOBLENZ presented its own problem for the drivers because the trucks were operating with only blackout lights rather that full headlights and taillights. To keep from being spotted by the enemy, blackout lights showed only a small slot of light, about an inch high by three inches wide, enough light to show drivers the small block of taillight of the vehicle in front of them. Consequently, the driver needed to stay close enough to the truck ahead to keep track of the blackout lights.

Their convoy of vehicles was stopped by American troops at a checkpoint, and the men were warned about Nazi soldiers who had crossed the front and were posing as American GIs, complete with stolen uniforms, jeeps, and identification. Consequently, numerous checkpoints had been set up to weed out any possible Nazis. Wilson and his men were asked one of the standard checkpoint questions—"Who won the World Series?" or "What's Sinatra's first name?" or some other question about American culture—and were allowed to continue the journey home.

As Wilson noted, a truck driver "didn't have the luxury of looking at the scenery to relax since the night was as black as it could be with no moonlight." It's no wonder that Wilson and the other drivers were exhausted after focusing on the blackout taillights of the truck in front of them for three hours. The drive turned out to be a tense way to end a week of deception activities. As Wilson noted, he was sound asleep as soon as his head the pillow at around three in the morning.

Five hours after the men of the Twenty-Third left the area where they had acted out Operation KOBLENZ, the Germans began a massive counteroffensive, a move that General Eisenhower called a "final, desperate blow into which every available reserve was thrown." The Germans called their last offensive attack of the war WATCH ON THE RHINE (December 16, 1944–January 25, 1945). It was a "cunning title" because if Allied code breakers came across it in intercepted German transmissions, they would more than likely believe that the buildup of troops was for a "fierce defense of the Rhine River, the last major physical barrier facing the Allies on their intended push into the heart of the Third Reich." It was, of course, much more than that.

The Allies called it the Ardennes Counteroffensive. But in the newspapers of the day, and later in history books, it became known as the Battle of the Bulge because the American press noted how the battlefield maps appearing regularly in newspapers showed a geographical bulge in the Allied front lines as the Germans attacked. However, it's more appropriate to call the Nazi offensive the *Battles* of the Bulge, since numerous battles raged during the frigid winter of 1944–1945.

The plan of the German army—with two hundred thousand troops, one thousand tanks and assault guns, and nineteen hundred artillery pieces—was to fight its way through the middle of the Allied front lines and push all the way to the port of Antwerp, Belgium. This push created a "bulge" in the Allied lines. Such a move, if successful, would capture the busiest Allied port. But, more important for the war effort, if the Nazi troops could break the Allied line in Ardennes and rush northwest to Antwerp, Hitler believed "all the northern Allied armies would be cut off and destroyed." With that victory, the German army would then pivot to the east and put an end to the Russian offensive.

With his plan to attack the heart of the American front lines, Hitler was counting on a repeat of the decisive German victory in the Ardennes region of Belgium in 1940, when the

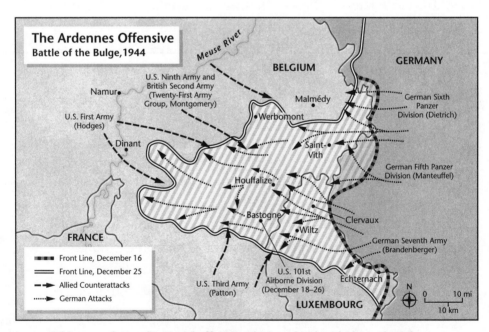

This map shows the Nazis' offensive designed to break through and divide the Allied front lines in the December 1944 Battle of the Bulge.

PANZER BRIGADE 150

A key part of Hitler's offensive was a deception called Operation GREIF (December 16–28, 1944), a special operation that would run in tandem with the massive Panzer offensive. GREIF was a false-flag deception, an operation that might include wearing enemy uniforms and operating captured enemy tanks and armored vehicles. His operation would include three parts, all secret actions behind enemy lines. First, the capture of at least two bridges across the Meuse River by "disguised raiding parties." Second, the "prompt reinforcement" of any such attack by armored commandos. Third, "an organized attempt to create confusion in the Allied rear areas through sabotage carried out by jeep parties clad in American uniforms."

The leader of the operation, Lieutenant Colonel Otto Skorzeny, had a "considerable reputation as a daring commando leader." He was given "unlimited powers to prepare his mission." He immediately began recruiting German soldiers and pilots who spoke English to be part of the unit called Panzer Brigade 150, "numbering about two thousand men, of whom 150 could speak English." All the recruits had to sign a pledge that stated, "Everything I know about the commitment of the 150th Panzer-Brigade is secret. . . . Breach of the order is punishable by death."

Since the cornerstone of the deception was being able to

Nazi Lieutenant Colonel Otto Skorzeny, leader of Panzer Brigade 150

pass as Americans, the men in the 150 watched hours of American movies and news reports "to learn the idiom, such as 'chow-line,' and to improve their accent." In addition, they spent "two hours a day on language and American customs, including how to eat 'with the fork after laying down the knife.'" Of course, the men were also taught commando skills, such as hand-to-hand combat training, demolition, and the use of enemy weapons.

The commandos were sent out in teams of three to six men to work behind American lines. Demolition squads were prepared to blow up bridges, ammunition dumps, and fuel depots. Reconnaissance patrols were to pass on fake orders to U.S. units they encountered, reverse road signs, and remove minefield warnings. The lead commando units disrupted the American chain of command by destroying telephone wires and radio stations, and issuing false orders.

While some of the operations behind enemy lines were disruptive, Panzer Brigade 150 never accomplished its overall goals. For one thing, Skorzeny had only five or six weeks to prepare. It was especially difficult for German troops, even those with knowledge of English, to master the language well enough to fool GIs who were born and raised in the United States.

Another reason that Panzer Brigade 150 was unsuccessful was that it couldn't get all the equipment it needed for its various operations. For example, while GREIF needed "20 Sherman tanks, 30 American armored cars, nearly 200 trucks, and 150 jeeps, Skorzeny got just two Shermans (one of which soon broke down), four armored cars, and about 30 jeeps," equipment that was stolen by German agents or damaged vehicles that were repaired by the agents. The rest of the equipment was German pieces, refurbished with sheet metal and a coat of olive-drab paint and the white U.S. star insignia. Even Skorzeny admitted that the fake tanks and personnel carriers would fool only "very young American troops, seeing them from very far away at night." It's no wonder that the Panzer Brigade 150 was unable to accomplish its goals.

Members of Panzer Brigade 150 are prepared for execution.

German army attacked the Allies in the Ardennes Forest and pushed them through France, where many of them needed to be evacuated at Dunkirk. This offensive—described by one World War II historian as "a great mishmash"—was not supported by the entire German High Command. Nevertheless, the Führer ignored any dissent and pushed on with his plan, a plan he knew *must* work to save his Third Reich.

In the meantime, Luxembourg City had changed dramatically since the men of the Twenty-Third had returned from KOBLENZ and while the Battle of the Bulge raged. Instead of being "the dullest part of the Western Front," the area became the portal for the U.S. Army divisions that were rushed there to stop the German army that exploded across the front. Luxembourg City was packed with soldiers streaming through on their way to the various battles that were part of the Battle of the Bulge offensive.

Although the Twenty-Third Headquarters company would remain in Luxembourg City, the deception units of the Twenty-Third had to vacate their base. The danger to the city wasn't that severe, but the "arrival of thousands of fighting reinforcements necessitated the evacuation of all Twenty-Third units." They moved "ignominiously westward to some cold, dirty flophouse barracks" in Doncourt, France. Fox gives the "official chronology" of what the men needed to do to protect the secret nature of the unit before they departed:

> *Organization alerted, documents and records placed in vehicles under guard for immediate departure. Rubber items and special equipment prepared for fire. Guard doubled. Machine gun*

nests set up for defense of sector surrounding bil-
lets. Attacked by air; Twenty-Third gunners posted
on roofs fired at enemy planes during
entire night.

Fox also made sure to note what was left out of the official report, namely "the enthusiasm with which those guns
were fired," since, as he put it, "it was the first and last time
they were . . . shot at the enemy."

When the Twenty-Third evacuated Luxembourg City,
there were still months of fighting ahead for the Allied
forces. As it turned out, the main role of the Twenty-Third
in the chaos of the Battle of the Bulge was to cover for units
that needed to be shifted to more strategic positions, particularly as the momentum of the battle swung toward the
Allies and the Nazis' attack literally ran out of gas. The work
of the Twenty-Third was especially crucial during a stretch
of cloudy and snowy days that grounded the army air corps
from hammering the Nazi advance until it had created a
bulge in the Allied front lines.

From December 22, 1944, until February 1, 1945, the
deception unit was involved in seven operations. In fact,
before the men could reach their new billet, the Signal
Company Special was called into action. Operation KODAK
(December 22–23) was to last only twenty-four hours and
was seen as "an attempt to confuse the enemy by present-
ing them a 'double-exposure' of our order of battle," using
spoof radio alone. The twenty-nine signalmen in the operation were guarded by a security detail of one hundred men
from the 406th. The Twenty-Third would show the Eightieth
Infantry and the Fourth Armored Division to be slightly

northeast of Luxembourg City, in a position to block any German plans to extend their attack to the southwest. While the Twenty-Third was simulating the notional divisions, the Fourth Infantry Division was preparing to move north to relieve the beleaguered troops in Bastogne. The Eightieth was preparing to attack from a spot north of Luxembourg City.

The Twenty-Third's signalmen manned twenty-nine radios, transmitting bogus messages that would lead the Germans to believe that both units were being held in reserve northeast of Luxembourg City at Echternach, a crucial river crossing. The real radio transmissions would show the division racing toward battle, creating a "double bluff" in a sense, hiding the movement of two real units critically needed elsewhere by giving the Germans two sets of radio transmissions, forcing them to decide which messages were coming from the real units.

The double bluff of KODAK gave the Allies the cover to send reinforcements to Bastogne, units that the Germans were led to believe were in Luxembourg, only to have them show up in Belgium to save their brothers in arms from the fearsome Panzer attack.

Lieutenant Fox, who took a great deal of pride in his band of actors and artists, did not think highly of KODAK: "The brevity of the operation and the confused tactical situation made it impractical to produce a polished reproduction of the Fourth or the Eightieth." As usual, there was no proof that the operation was a success. Nevertheless, the units that were covered by the deception surprised the Germans when they arrived at their destinations.

For some of the men, Christmas came early, with a

dramatic and long-awaited improvement in the weather. E. Gordon Wilson remembered waking up on December 23 to a "beautiful, clear day and the wonderful sight of hundreds of bombers flying over." He noted that it had been a week since the army air corps planes could fly critical support missions. Wilson recalled planes "as far as we could see to the north of us."

The men of the Twenty-Third knew what the clear weather meant to the fighting troops. The "glittering formations" of planes would "methodically destroy the long columns of Germans—first as they advanced, then as they retreated, abandoning their tanks for lack of gas, trudging home through the slushy mud." The Fifth and Sixth Panzer Divisions were destroyed by the air attacks. Seeing the waves of planes heading east, Ed Biow remembered thinking that "things were getting the way they should be." And

In the Night Fog Moving into the Bulge, a painting by Robert N. Blair

Lieutenant Fox wrote to his wife, Hannah, "For the first time since I joined the war, I like the idea of Germans being blown to hell."

While the men may have been elated by the resumption of U.S. bombing, Fox felt that "Christmas was a very sad day for everyone." It's not hard to imagine why the men of the Twenty-Third felt that way. Not long before the Nazi offensive, American troops had visions of a war that would be over before Christmas and the men home with their loved ones. That was not to be. In addition to false rumors about the end of the war, the weather was frigid and dreary. Snow had begun to fall before KODAK and stayed on the ground for well over a month. And the men were living in filthy and cold "flophouse barracks."

Despite the wretched conditions and being far from home, some of the men were not deterred from celebrating Christmas. Harold Dahl, one of the artists of the 603rd, had fond memories of the Christmas of 1944. In a letter to his parents, he wrote how he and some of the men in the camouflage unit were so touched by their impromptu celebration that they had tears in their eyes. Biow, a truck driver in the camouflage engineers, remembered what some of his unit did for the celebration. Somebody cut a small tree, and they made Christmas decorations "out of anything, stars cut out of the tops of tin cans, and it was so damn cold I smoked the first cigar I ever smoked in my life in some desperate attempt to get warm."

The Christmas spirit of the men of the Twenty-Third led them to show compassion for about a dozen disconsolate families of "displaced persons" who lived in a nearby village. The families that had moved into abandoned buildings

U.S. tank men try to stay warm on Christmas Day.

were primarily from Eastern European countries, such as Russia, Czechoslovakia, Poland, and Hungary. These DPs, as they were called, were refugees and escapees from Nazi slave labor camps who'd been liberated by the advancing Allied troops.

The men of the Twenty-Third saw a heartbreaking sight. The people were "pale and gaunt, many were sickly. They lived on the barest scraps of food and huddled together at night for warmth. Most had no more possessions than the ragged clothes they were wearing." They were the "refuse of the war—the human wreckage of the Blitzkrieg and the slave camps."

The American soldiers decided to share the bounty of their packages from home with these desperate people. The men were especially touched by the children among these "displaced persons" and decided to host a Christmas party. Each family received a package of goodies, including "rations, candy, crackers, kids' clothes sent from home, socks, blankets, even lemon juice and sugar lumps for medicine against sore throats." Each child got his or her own "little package of Christmas treats, mainly candy, gum, ribbons, and small toys." The Americans sang Christmas songs in English, and the children returned the favor by singing songs in their own languages.

For that brief time, the men of the Twenty-Third "did their modest part in bringing humanity back to a world ruined by war—by making a bunch of kids happy." In a letter to his parents, Richard H. Morton wrote how the children who received gifts from the members of his unit were "absolutely speechless—as nothing had been done for them in so long. The children had never seen candy before."

Rather than spending Christmas with his unit, Lieutenant Fox had been in Luxembourg City with the rest of the command staff. He wrote to his wife, "Most of the church bells rang twelve. Way out in the valley we heard some lonely trumpeters blow 'O Holy Night.'" But that mood of tranquility was soon broken by the war. On the drive back to the city, air raid sirens sounded.

On the day after Christmas, most of the unit arrived in Verdun, France, and settled into what Fox called "a very dirty and windy" French military barracks in a "depressing city filled with a million ghosts of other unhappy soldiers. That makes it much too crowded." He was referring to the horrific World War I battle of Verdun, which raged for ten months, exemplifying "the grinding, bloody nature of warfare on the Western Front" during that drawn-out conflict.

While the change in billet gave the artists of the 603rd a chance to explore new panoramas, the move didn't mean that much to Bill Blass. While most of the artists spent their free time sketching local scenes and other men in the unit, Blass continued to fill his sketchbooks with his visions of women's fashion. He often managed to get his hands on a fashion magazine that he kept close by, even when he was in a foxhole.

One of the members of the unit admitted that, while most of the men were "a bunch of slobs," Blass usually found a way to iron his uniform. Sergeant Bob Tompkins remembered him as "very flamboyant, very outgoing, very cheerful." Tompkins thought enough of Blass that Tompkins chose Blass to be the godfather of his son born while the Twenty-Third was in France. And another member of the unit remarked that Blass never took the easy way out of an assignment.

The next two weeks saw the Twenty-Third in action in two operations: METZ I (December 28–31, 1944) and METZ II (January 6–9, 1945). The objective of METZ I was to "cover the non-secret movement of the Eighty-Seventh Infantry Division when it came up to Reims to take part in the attack of the Nazi bulge." It was a "small effort by less than two hundred special effects men. A little spoof radio [unit] was donated by the 3103rd Signal Service Battalion."

ARTISTS OF THE 603RD: BILL BLASS

While other artists of the 603rd, like Arthur Singer and Ellsworth Kelly, began their long and successful artistic careers as children drawing songbirds and cats, Bill Blass started on his artistic path at age fifteen by selling sketches of evening gowns that he envisioned at his home in Fort Wayne, Indiana, "a miserable place to grow up in." Although Blass's early life coincided with the Great Depression, he was "captivated by the glamour of movies and fashion magazines." The young Blass "filled the margins of his schoolbooks with drawings of Hollywood-inspired fashions" and sold sketches of his designs to fashion houses in New York City.

When Blass saved up enough money from selling his sketches, he left Indiana in 1939 and settled in New York City, where he began studying fashion at Parsons School of Design. He soon found a job as a sketch artist for a sportswear company. So talented was the young Blass that he was the first man to win *Mademoiselle* magazine's Design for Living Award, a high honor from a prestigious fashion publication.

Blass returned to the world of fashion in New York after serving with the *camoufleurs* of the 603rd. Working as a designer at some of the city's most influential fashion houses, his reputation grew with the success of the companies. Finally, in 1970 he created Bill Blass Limited and designed dresses and suits for some of America's most famous women, including Hollywood stars and First Ladies.

Blass's company grew as he expanded his brand. The marketplace saw new Bill Blass products from swimwear to furs, bed linens to perfumes, luggage to chocolate. In fact, in 1989 Blass shared his talents with the Ford Motor Company for an exclusive Bill Blass edition of the high-end Continental Mark series of cars.

In 1993, three years before his death, Bill Blass sold his company for $50 million and retired to his estate in Connecticut. His will included a gift of half of his $52-million estate and several important ancient sculptures to the Metropolitan Museum of Art. Before he retired, Blass shared his wealth with the community. In 1994, he donated $10 million to the New York Public Library, which created the Bill Blass Public Catalog Room.

The man who went from sketching dresses in Indiana to being considered by many to be the "Dean of American Designers" lived his life believing that the "beauty of being able to draw, to paint, from an early age is that you never feel trapped, least of all by your immediate circumstances."

The day after the arrival of the Twenty-Third was filled with their normal special-effects protocol to create a notional Eighty-Seventh Headquarters in Metz. They sewed on shoulder patches and painted the phony bumper markings on their vehicles. The men put up fifty directional signs, pointing the way to various units of the Eighty-Seventh, none of which, of course, were near Metz. Since no signs indicated the way to the command post, MPs were not necessary. The men carefully staged activities that enemy agents would look for: soldiers moving about, trucks carrying troops to the water point and to the enlisted men's showers. By 11:15 that night, the special effects men moved out of the city to a wooded area to remove their uniform patches and bumper markings before heading back to Verdun.

Playing his part in the special effects deception of METZ I, Technician Fifth Grade E. Gordon Wilson was given the job of hauling the camp's trash to the local dump. As he approached the dump, he saw a large group of locals there in one area. Not wanting to get entangled with civilians, he drove his truck to another part of the dump. Wilson had barely emptied the first of his four GI cans—thirty to forty gallons each—when he was "surrounded by dozens of people grabbing, pushing and shoving to get at the food as it hit the ground." Some of the people held back the crowd while others helped Wilson empty his remaining cans. Wilson drove off a short distance and watched "as the crowd swarmed over the wet and soggy mess, grabbing for food."

Years later, he still remembered "in the maze of activity . . . a teenage boy reaching for a small plastic-wrapped package of soda crackers—not much of a food item I thought." He drove back to camp with an "entirely different feeling about the war. We had never missed a meal—even though many meals had been cold from a box or can. It really gave us something to think about. . . . I wondered just how much 'food' was really in our garbage."

Lieutenant Fox recalls that New Year's Eve, which occurred between METZ I and METZ II, wasn't a particularly festive time for his men or for him. "It is hard to celebrate," he wrote, "in dreary, cold, unlighted barracks." And it wasn't very long before he returned to Metz for METZ II. The objective of the deception was to use radio spoof to make it appear that the Ninetieth Infantry Division was holding in a reserve position in Metz until the Ninety-Fourth Infantry Division was in position. While the notional Ninetieth was in Metz, the genuine division was, in fact, on its way to reinforce the Americans at Bastogne.

Eleven radios of the Twenty-Third replaced the network of the Ninetieth for three to ten hours, but there was no message traffic and only the most infrequent call-ups. While the spoof radio network was in operation, other members of the unit carried out their usual special effects activities, acting on specific instructions on how to simulate the Ninetieth. Three-quarters of all the men were to wear helmets bearing the Ninetieth Division insignia, and all would wear the shoulder patch.

While Operation METZ II was considered a success by army intelligence, it came at a price, the first death of a member of the 3132nd Signal Service Company Special. Since there is no official account of the operation on record, it's hard to know what really happened to Technician Fifth Grade Chester Pellicioni. We do know that it was another frigid day and the men were cleaning out debris from the building that they had been using. Trying to get warm, the men built a fire in a cast-iron stove. Lieutenant Dick Syracuse was no more than thirty feet away from the stove when it exploded, killing Pellicioni. It's possible that the stove had been booby-trapped by the German troops who had occupied the building before the men from the Twenty-Third. There was speculation that the Nazis left a hand grenade in the stove, making it ready to explode the next time a fire was lit in it.

The shrapnel from the blast killed Pellicioni but injured no one else in the unit. So, after a dozen dangerous operations, the first member of the unit to die was a signalman, killed outside his own billet, where he felt safe. On that wickedly cold night, "the fabled luck of the Special Troops ran out." All the more reason why Fox considered METZ II "rather sloppy and unsatisfactory."

Following METZ II, the work of the Twenty-Third over the next three weeks included four shorter operations—L'EGLISE (January 10–13) and FLAXWEILER (January 17–18), as well as STEINSEL and LANDONVILLERS (both January 27–28)—that utilized a limited number of men.

The objective of L'EGLISE was to convince the Germans that the Fourth had moved into a reserve position near L'Église, Belgium. In reality, the Fourth had moved into an attack position east of Luxembourg City. The Twenty-Third would cover this move that would be made under a blackout. No dummies were used in this deception, since the area was already teeming with tanks. With all that tank noise, there was no need for the sonic trucks either. The radio traffic came from eighteen notional radios from mobile teams.

They drove back and forth between different combat areas to give the illusion of a number of radio stations.

The special effects called for establishing a fake Fourth Armored Division Headquarters, manned by the special effects players at a beautiful mansion. Fox recalled that the weather was "frightfully cold but the snow was lovelier than the finest Belgian lace. Everyone was snugly billeted." Their comfortable quarters didn't last very long, however, as the unit returned to its base at Briey, France, after a few days.

The Twenty-Third was barely back at Briey when the sonic unit raced up to the Moselle River, east of Luxembourg City, for a one-night deception near the town in Luxembourg that gave the deception its name. Operation FLAXWEILER provided the men of the Twenty-Third the chance to do "what they did best: simulating a river crossing." This time the sonic show was performed twenty miles south of where the real attackers would cross the Our River. The quality of the Twenty-Third's response was a "good example of how quickly the 3132nd could put their prerecorded library of sounds to work."

The Second Cavalry Group managed the special effects in FLAXWEILER, increasing reconnaissance and displaying bridge-making material and boats. The 3132nd added heavy equipment sounds to the work of the Second as the sonic trucks drove up and down a road near the river. In the morning, the 3132nd slipped out of harm's way and returned to its billet at Briey.

At the end of January, the Twenty-Third ran two concurrent operations, each featuring a small part of the unit. Recently promoted to captain, Fox was in command of

Operation STEINSEL, "one of the most economical [operations] ever attempted," involving seventy-two enlisted men, four officers, and twenty-two vehicles in a radio-only deception. STEINSEL was similar to ELSENBORN in that it involved the radio operators of the Twenty-Third's Signal Company Special infiltrating spoof radio with the Fourth Infantry Division network. The men began their infiltration two days before the start of the full spoof-radio program. Since the Twenty-Third and the Fourth had worked together before, the transition to spoof radio went smoothly.

Fox praised something near and dear to the hearts of the men of the Twenty-Third: the tasty food provided by the division. On this short operation, his men didn't bring any food because there were "plenty of warm messes [dining halls] in the area and people ate wherever they happened to be." Technician Fifth Grade Wilson wrote that he "had come to look forward to the good food I always had" while working with the Fourth.

While some of the men of the Twenty-Third were working on STEINSEL, others were busy with Operation LANDONVILLERS, which was practically identical to METZ II. It was even in the same geographical area. In this deception, the Ninety-Fifth Infantry Division was to be replaced by the Twenty-Sixth Infantry Division. The signalmen simulated the Ninety-Fifth with spoof radio alone, holding the division in position for twelve to twenty-four hours during a "dangerous transition," that is, while the Ninety-Fifth was leaving and the Twenty-Sixth was taking its place. Both infantry divisions moved under blackout conditions and pulled off the change without being attacked in the vulnerable time.

The deception was completed with special effects, which

included giving the vehicles in the operation a whitewash of snow camouflage, to match the genuine vehicles of the Ninety-Fifth. Even though the entire operation lasted just a couple of days, the command was taking no chances with security, ordering the men to burn all letters so they didn't give away the real identity of the unit.

This type of operation—spoof radio with special effects—was becoming standard operational practice for the Twenty-Third. The final report noted that the "degree of success was unknown." Nevertheless, the men of the Twenty-Third must have felt a sense of accomplishment with the precision and coordination of the operation, as they continued to make it possible for combat units to return to battle, often to support their brothers in arms in need of reinforcements.

CHAPTER 8

AFTER THE BATTLE OF THE BULGE

Like many of the frontline soldiers, the men of the Twenty-Third had hoped that the war would be over by Christmas of 1944 and they would safely return to their homes. Unfortunately, they were "doomed to disappointment [as] the German war machine was still not destroyed." In fact, the Nazi fighting spirit seemed as fierce as ever. "The beast fought blindly on" as the enemy moved closer to the homeland.

In the east, the Russians crossed into German territory for the first time in the war, marching into Hungary and Yugoslavia, Poland and parts of East Prussia. In the west, the Allies were on the offensive and taking back territory they had lost in the Battle of the Bulge, clearing France and Belgium. In addition, their supply lines had improved when the Allies had successfully taken control of Antwerp and its crucial harbor.

Three army groups were coming closer to the Rhine:

- The Twenty-First Army Group, under the command of Field Marshal Montgomery, included the First U.S. Army and the Ninth U.S. Army.
- The Twelfth Army Group, under the command of General Bradley, included the First U.S. Army and the Third U.S. Army.
- The Sixth Army Group, under the command of General Jacob Devers, included the Seventh U.S. Army and First French Army.

Supreme Allied Commander Eisenhower planned to move his troops into position to cross the Rhine and drive into Germany. In the meantime, as the Allied soldiers continued to fight their way to the Rhine, the Twenty-Third played its part in getting those armies into position for the Rhine assault in March.

Inflatable dummy vehicles in France, 1945

The Twenty-Third began February 1945 with Operation WHIPSAW, a deception that included simultaneous operations. Once again, the objective was to draw German troops to a place on the front and hold them there for a brief time, in this case by creating the presence of a buildup of Third Army infantry and armored units. There would be no special effects or spoof radio, although the 3132nd provided its usual legitimate communications.

The first part of WHIPSAW (February 1–4, 1945) involved the sonic company simulating tank activity along the Moselle River, painting "the picture of three tank battalions adjusting their positions and establishing outposts" at three different locations in Germany. The first show of the night of February 1 simulated tanks converging near Grevenmacher, Luxembourg. The next night they repeated the program at Wormeldingen, also in Luxembourg. On the final night of the three shows, they projected the sounds of random tank maneuvers in both areas.

Judging from the number of reconnaissance flights over the area, the Germans seemed "clearly . . . taken by the ruse." The command of the Twenty-Third was surprised; the Germans wouldn't risk so many aircraft reconnaissance flights in an area unless they were concerned about it. Of course the sonic company took this as a sign of the success of its sonic shows.

The Luftwaffe planes flooded the region with flares, which were but a prelude to what would come next. The Germans opened up on the area with two of their most dreaded and lethal weapons, mortar and 88mm artillery fire. Nevertheless, by 9:30 p.m. on February 3, after the barrage, the sonic company had packed up and returned to Briey.

The Second Cavalry Group did its part in the operation, "adding to the local activity by shifting its tanks about in visible locations, displaying bridge building equipment, and increasing its patrolling." They also got some local artillery units to shoot more so-called "registration salvos." While these registration shots may have seemed random to most soldiers, to experienced artillerymen, they were an indication that an attack was in the works.

For one thing, such artillery shots frequently showed where an attack would be coming from based on where the artillery was set up to support the attack. Infantry and armored units could arrive at an area and quickly be ready for battle. Artillerymen, on the other hand, needed time to set up and figure out where they wanted their shells to land. They figured this by firing, in a sense, practice rounds to double-check their calculations and map work, studying where a round was aimed and where it actually hit. As for the enemy, the registration rounds indicated that a new artillery unit had moved into an area to support the ground troops who would be part of the attack.

To support the artillery fire, most of the men of the 603rd and 406th convoyed from Briey on the morning of February 3. By early afternoon they were at Saarlautern, Germany, setting up two battalions of artillery decoys. They chose a spot that had been used by a previous artillery unit, so the ground was covered with telltale tracks—visible by aerial reconnaissance—of a genuine artillery battalion. Because the ground was frozen, the men of the Twenty-Third would not have time to dig in during their short time there.

Technician Fifth Grade Wilson tells the story of an incident related to the inflated artillery pieces, a story told to him by one of the radio operators in his unit. The policy of the Twenty-Third had long been to prevent anyone who wasn't part of the Twenty-Third from getting close to the decoys, and that included officers. On this particular night, an American colonel approached the radio operator, who was guarding some inflated artillery dummies. The officer was able to see the guns in the distance and, not knowing they were fake, told the guard that the long barrel of one artillery piece looked a bit droopy. The guard "said something like, 'No, sir, it must be the heat waves or atmospheric conditions that make it look that way.'" The guard and the colonel went back and forth about "atmospheric conditions" before the officer walked off, "still possibly unconvinced." The guard immediately called a repair crew that inflated the gun to its proper pressure.

The decoy artillery pieces were left in position from one a.m. on February 4 until nightfall of the next day, to make sure the Germans had a good chance to see them. After

A dummy artillery piece

their "show," the engineers and *camoufleurs* packed up their decoys, loaded their trucks, and drove back to their billet at Briey.

Operation MERZIG (February 13–14, 1945) was another sonic deception operation of the Twenty-Third, a type of deception that "was becoming more popular." This one was designed to keep the Eleventh Panzer Division where it was so it couldn't bring its fierce tank attack to a weaker area of the front line. The Twelfth Army Group knew that the Panzer division was in position at Remich, Luxembourg, opposite the U.S. Ninety-Fourth Infantry Division, and felt they were "fairly harmless" where they were.

MERZIG called for the sonic company to simulate a gathering of tanks in the XX sector near the town of Merzig, Germany. The sonic program was to fill the air on two consecutive nights. The Third Cavalry Group lent its assistance by moving some of its tanks around in an area known to be under Nazi observation, and in general by increasing the amount of movement, fire, and activity in the area.

During both nights of the operation, Nazi reconnaissance planes flew over the area every hour, dropping flares. The enemy also dropped in "135 rounds of 80mm mortar and 28 rounds of artillery." U.S. intelligence officers found the bombardment unusual since the Germans were said to be running out of ammunition and limiting their shells to definite targets. Also unusual was the extensive activity of Luftwaffe planes in the area, since the Twenty-Third had not used decoys very often, relying instead on special effects to dupe local Nazi agents and sympathizers.

The men of the sonic company spent two frightening nights under that heavy German bombardment, "the one experience that none of them ever forgot, a sense of fated helplessness, the world exploding first in front, then behind, then a hundred yards away. They could not shoot back." The Germans held their ground, in what was a defensive position.

The Twenty-Third returned to home base on February 16. The after-action report mentioned one of the possible benefits of the deception program at Merzig was that the Germans believed there was a large number of tanks on the other side of the river and had given up more easily than if they'd known they were up against but a handful of light tanks from the Third Cavalry Group.

Despite the fact that the men of the deception unit were not part of a frontline unit, they were, in fact, never very far from danger and death. Years later, Dave Wynshaw said that he "can still hear machine guns. I can still hear artillery at night. There are times when I'm sitting . . . and I hear it. I hear it. They're not shooting at me, but I hear it. It's indelible."

One risk that the men of the Twenty-Third faced arose from the fact that so many of their missions at this point in the war were staged near Luxembourg City. Would any of them be recognized as the same troops that locals and soldiers from the regular army had seen on previous occasions, this time wearing different shoulder patches? Lieutenant Dick Syracuse, of the 3132nd's security detail, had an outgoing and friendly personality that made him a memorable sort of guy. Some of the other troops began to recognize him, and noticed him wearing a shoulder patch from a different outfit every few weeks. The lieutenant's "quick-thinking response was to tell them that he really must be a screw-up as he kept getting bounced from unit to unit."

The next deception had all the complications of an elaborate football play. LOCHINVAR (March 1–11, 1945) was conceived to cover the movement of three divisions on the Saar River front lines. First of all, the battle-weary Ninety-Fourth Infantry Division was to be relieved by the Twenty-Sixth Infantry Division on its immediate right. The empty spot in the line left by the Twenty-Sixth was to be filled by the Sixty-Fifth, which had just arrived from the United States.

Part of the reason for the complicated situation was to ease the inexperienced troops of the Sixty-Fifth Infantry Division into the war, a common practice for the U.S. Command. The reasoning made sense. Should the green troops suffer a high number of casualties in their initial taste of battle, many of the troops could be psychologically damaged. Making the swap in LOCHINVAR might give

TRENCH ART

When the Twenty-Third settled in Luxembourg City, all but the sonic unit billeted on the north side of the city. The Twenty-Third's Headquarters and Service Company factory section also set up shop nearby and was manned by "talented machinists who could [make] gun parts and just about anything else the Special Troops needed." These men also fashioned all sorts of "trench art," objects made from the debris of battle, like 76mm Sherman tank shells cut down into ashtrays.

Most experts agree that trench art began during the Napoleonic Wars of 1799–1815, when prisoners of war were allowed to sell items they made from wood or bone "to subsidize their meager rations." The practice continued in the Crimean War (1853–1856) — between the Russian Empire and an alliance of England, France, and the Ottoman Empire — the "first war where 'on the spot' journalism could take place," with reports telegraphed back to England, where they appeared in British newspapers a few days after the battlefield action they described. England's victory created a market for souvenirs of the war, "with impoverished locals collecting debris from battlefields and forging them into inkwells and mementos to sell to English tourists and traders."

Although the practice of crafting battlefield souvenirs became more popular during the wars at the end of the 1800s,

An example of trench art: engraved artillery shells

it rose to a new level of popularity in World War I, when developments in weapon technology introduced breach-loaded artillery, which produced the brass shells and cartridge casings that became the staples of trench art. In addition, "bullets, aluminum, buttons, shrapnel, empty ammunition clips . . . were picked up off of the battlefields and became . . . artistic assemblages or souvenirs." Some soldiers created smaller items such as rings. And wounded soldiers were encouraged to utilize this type of art as part of their therapy.

Although soldiers continued to take and make souvenirs—Harold Dahl, one of the artists of the Twenty-Third, was a fan of military weapons—the practice of creating trench art from battlefield debris dwindled in World War II, when armies no longer spent months in trenches. The armies of World War II were more mobile, enjoying little of the downtime needed to create trench art. However, the artists of the Twenty-Third were mobile artists, ready to grab their art supplies whenever there was a lull in their activities and create images that captured the scenes and moods of the European ground war.

the new soldiers some time to adjust until they had gained more experience on the front lines.

Although two dozen of the signalmen found themselves under fire, Technician Fifth Grade Wilson remembers two days of taking it easy. "Nothing to do but relax in the sun," he wrote, "camping on the side of a high hill—just the three of us on my team—the war in the distance but nobody shooting at us and nobody giving orders . . . a good book to read—and plenty of time to sleep if we wanted."

Wilson and his crew remained in position until it was time to shut down their radios and pack up their equipment. A lieutenant showed up in a jeep and told them to follow him in their truck. As Wilson recalled, he drove for miles as fast as he could, following the jeep, but after some time, the soldiers realized that the lieutenant had gotten lost, as they had arrived at the front lines. The men were quickly chased away by U.S. troops who were fearful that the newcomers would draw enemy fire to their position.

The officer's jeep stopped, then raced ahead, then stopped again. Wilson wondered if the lieutenant needed time to think about "how close he came to getting his tailfeathers clipped" by the enemies' deadly 88mm artillery gun. Wilson's truck pulled off the road until they got a radio message to await instructions.

As the sky darkened and the temperature dropped, the men decided to see if they could warm themselves in a nearby house. The French family there proved to be quite friendly and invited the men into their home. The wife was in the middle of cooking dinner and immediately put three more venison steaks on the fire. When the lieutenant and his driver arrived, she added two more steaks. Soon, all the men "sat around in this little stone house. . . . This Army invasion of this little family didn't seem to bother them in the least."

Finally, the lieutenant received word that they needed to move out. Wilson and his team were the last to leave. However, as they prepared to return to the billet, Wilson realized that the men had "much food, chocolate and soap scattered in [the] truck," leftover items from their 10-in-1 boxes. They gathered these goodies and "left a large pile of dry and canned food, chocolate and soap in [the] front yard and hurried to catch up with the others."

Leaving in such a rush, Wilson didn't have time to tell the family of their farewell gift. The signalman often wondered if the family used the items they had left piled in the yard. He hoped "this repaid them in some way for all those wonderful venison steaks they did not have for their family to eat."

The Twenty-Third's role in LOCHINVAR was to fool the Nazis into believing that the Ninety-Fourth and Twenty-Sixth were merely swapping sectors. However, the Sixty-Fifth was to hide with the Ninety-Fourth and wear Ninety-Fourth patches. The vehicles of the newly arrived infantrymen were to be marked with 94-X, meaning Ninety-Fourth Infantry Division. The radio operators of the Signal Company Special were to infiltrate the radio networks of the Ninety-Fourth and move down into the spot where the Sixty-Fifth was supposed to be. While all this swapping and playacting was going on, the Ninety-Fourth was to go into the reserve position and get its well-deserved rest.

What actually happened, however, was quite different. The Nazis, aware that some troop movement was going on, took what Fox called the "unstable situation" and attacked, putting LOCHINVAR into a "small tailspin." The Ninety-Fourth—partially on the front line, partially in reserve—returned to its original position. In the confusion and attack, two of the Signal Company Special's radios were damaged by artillery fire. Two other radio teams were cut off by the Germans for about forty-eight hours.

The next operation, which wound up being the next-to-last operation of the Twenty-Third, was "one of the shortest operations on record." Operation BOUZONVILLE (March 11–13, 1945) lasted only thirty-three hours, but it had the tragic distinction of being the "deadliest show they ever staged," leaving two men dead and fifteen wounded. The deception was designed to draw attention away from the main effort of XX Corps between Trier and Saarburg, Germany, by showing troops lined up farther south opposite Saarlautern. On the morning of the real attack, March 12, the Sixty-Fifth Infantry Division was to put on a demonstration enhanced by the Twenty-Third's rubber guns and flash devices.

On March 11, spoof radio went live requesting periodic checks. The *camoufleurs* set up their dummy artillery with the batteries that allowed the men to coordinate their flash fires with the firing by the Sixty-Fifth Division Artillery. Seven teams of men wearing the markings of the Eightieth Infantry appeared in surrounding towns and villages. The playacting was completed with MPs at strategic checkpoints, while bogus command posts and road signs pointed to the presence of the notional Eightieth.

Dave Wynshaw remembered how scary it was for some of the men doing guard duty near the notional encampment. "We were stuck on top of a hill, silhouetted against the sky," he said. "They couldn't miss us, but they did. Artillery was firing and we couldn't move. And I know it must have been four, six hours that we were stuck there." Wynshaw was overwhelmed by one emotion: "Fear. Fear. Everything you're doing is fear."

Around noon on March 12, a group of twenty-three men operating near Picard, Germany, came under artillery fire, the same sort of random attacks that had become more common of late. There was "nothing special about this shelling, which appeared to be typical harassing fire." A common German artillery practice was to drop their shells on roads and at crossroads. And, as signalman Wilson put it, "if you just happened to be passing, it could be the end of that trip." In this instance, the random shelling killed Captain Thomas G. Wells and Staff Sergeant George C. Peddle, and left thirteen men wounded, including two officers.

For Technician Fifth Grade Wilson, "the best way to handle this kind of situation in a war is to try to forget it—to hush it up—to get on with the job because nobody knows what the next day will bring." Frederic Fox, especially close to Wells, couldn't easily block out his friend's death. "Even in a fake play," Fox wrote after the war, "a runner can get hurt. I lost a friend [during BOUZONVILLE]. . . . As Tom was riding in the front seat of his jeep, a German shell burst in the tree directly overhead and ripped his throat in half." Wells was "making traffic," a common special effects activity, something many of the men in the Twenty-Third had done. In this case, Wells was "building up vehicular movement for the phony Eightieth. . . . driving back and forth along the tree-lined roads on the west bank of the Moselle."

Two months after Wells's death, Fox wrote a letter of condolence to his friend's widow, telling her, "I can think of no

ARTISTS OF THE 603RD:
HAROLD LAYNOR

When Harold "Hal" Laynor was a kid, he collected stamps. The hobby gave him a chance to learn geography and instilled a keen interest in travel. One of the places he wanted to visit as a boy was Paris. When he was twelve years old, he swapped his stamp collection for an oil painting set and began to concentrate on art. He now dreamed about going to Paris one day to study art. Laynor would eventually get to the City of Lights—but not in the way he had imagined.

As a young man, Laynor studied at Parsons School of Design in New York; he also took various painting jobs to gain experience and develop his craft. At one such job, "he painted neckties for a small factory in Harlem—Statue of Liberty, hula girls, whatever they wanted." He also worked for a famous New York department store adding the skies on landscape paintings that the store sold. Other members of his team added different elements to the paintings, such as a barn or a haystack.

Like a lot of young men of his generation, Laynor felt it was his duty to serve his country when the United States entered World War II. So, after studying graphic arts at Parsons, he went with his father to the army recruiting office in Greenwich Village and enlisted. Intrigued by the possibility of painting camouflage, he liked the idea that "he could use his sense of color and form for the war effort."

After seven months of combat, Laynor was seriously wounded in an enemy shelling during Operation BOUZONVILLE that killed one of the signalmen in his company. Medics discovered a chunk of shrapnel buried in Laynor's back. After surgery, Laynor recuperated in Paris. It was not the glamorous stay he might have imagined as a kid, but the experience did turn out to play a key role in his artistic education and development because while he was there, he had the good fortune to meet and spend time with the famous Spanish painter Pablo Picasso. Laynor wrote to his wife that visiting Picasso's studio and working with him "greatly inspires me to continue with my painting." Much later in his career, Laynor said that Picasso had a significant influence on his style.

Laynor admitted he had a "soft time" recovering in Paris. However, as he wrote in a letter to his parents, "Although I am having a heck of a good time here, doing art work and seeing Paris . . . I do really want to get back to the outfit." Such was the pull of friendship for the men of the Twenty-Third.

After the war, Laynor went back to school, getting a master's degree and later his doctorate in art. He enjoyed a long and successful career as an art professor and artist, pioneering the use of lacquer as a painting medium. Dr. Laynor was known for his unique painting techniques and his support of art education through three-dimensional painting for the blind and financial support for visual arts students and educators. His dedication to arts education led to the creation of the Laynor Foundation Museum.

Dr. Harold "Hal" Laynor died in 1991.

reason why the Lord would have wished to take him away from us—except perhaps that He wanted us to feel the cruel price of this war and the absolute necessity for living peaceful, generous lives."

Early in the evening of March 12, the sonic unit played one of its tank programs on the west side of the river, two miles north of Saarlautern. Spoof radio nets were also established, although they sent no messages. Special effects men playacted in the usual ways: shoulder patches worn, bumper markings displayed, trucks routed to bogus supply points, all under the watchful eyes of fake MPs. While the Twenty-Third established the presence of the notional Eightieth, the real Eightieth attacked the following morning under a customary security blackout.

Spoof radio transmissions ended at midnight on March 12. Soon, all the men involved in BOUZONVILLE faded away and drove back to the billet at Briey. The Eightieth reported light resistance, which pleased the XX Corps.

CHAPTER 9

THE FINAL DECEPTION

By the middle of January 1945, the Allies had regained the territory they had lost to the Germans during the Battle of the Bulge. While Berlin, Germany, was the ultimate objective of the Allied Command, the Ruhr River valley, "with its coal mines, blast furnaces, and factories, the muscle with which Germany waged war, was the more vital objective" as its next strategic target. Without the Ruhr, the Third Reich had no chance to survive. All would be lost as the mostly U.S. Army charged across the Rhine from the east while the Russians were bearing down from the west. As one military historian wrote, "It is difficult, in retrospect, to comprehend how any thinking German could have believed genuinely in anything other than defeat as 1945 opened."

As the Allies planned to cross the Rhine, things indeed looked grim for the once-invincible German troops. They were low on nearly everything they needed to continue the war: food, fuel, ammunition, battle-tested soldiers. And airplanes. One Nazi commander noted that the army was really a "shadow of an army." As the mood of the soldiers varied from "suspicion to callous resignation," the Nazi troops could only offer weak resistance. And after Allied bombers flew eight thousand sorties in the three days leading up to the Rhine crossing, the Luftwaffe nearly vanished from the skies over Germany.

It's small wonder that the morale of the Nazi soldiers was poor, as they were threatened with capital punishment if they did not fight to the end. Field commanders received orders from the German High Command that listed some of the "offenses" that merited execution of guilty soldiers: "failing to blow up a bridge on time, being related to a deserter, withdrawing without orders, failing to fight to the end." To guard against desertion, stragglers not with their units were to be executed. Luftwaffe General Albert Kesselring knew what was expected of him: "My orders are categorical. Hang on!"

The German army was prepared to take a stand—their final stand—on the east side of the Rhine River. Much of the fighting in the European theater had involved rivers and river crossings: the Seine, the Moselle, the Saar and the Maas, the Erft, the Ruhr, and, finally, the Rhine. But, as one historian noted, the Rhine was more than a river. It was the "source of weird and romantic legends . . . a historic moat" guarding the Germans from their enemies. The Allies saw it as the final obstacle standing between them and victory.

Before the Allies could roll on to Berlin and end the war, they needed to create a plan for crossing a river that "varied from 900 to 1,500 feet" across, a river that Supreme Allied Commander Dwight D. Eisenhower said was "not only wide but treacherous." To make matters worse for the troops preparing to cross the Rhine, the enemy could manipulate its current by opening dams on the river's eastern tributaries. To thwart such efforts, the Allies posted several detachments to guard the dams.

The plan for the assault, Operation PLUNDER (March 23–24, 1945), would involve traversing the river in a number of spots, a "monumental crossing . . . the largest amphibious operation since Normandy." To prepare for the assault at Wesel, Germany, the Allies had collected a massive amount of supplies. The Ninth Army had 138,000 tons of supplies for the crossing. The Second Army amassed sixty thousand tons of ammunition and thirty thousand tons of engineer stores. In addition to the supplies, "more than 37,000 British and 22,000 American engineers would participate in the assault." The Allies set a "world-record 66-mile-long smoke screen" along the west bank of the Rhine in attempt to hide their preparations. As Lieutenant Colonel Simenson later recalled, there were "a half million men crossing the Rhine, and it was just beautiful."

Just as Operation OVERLORD (1944) had deceived the Nazis about the landing at Normandy, the Allies planned a similar deception for the Rhine crossing, disguising the three key elements of the assault: the locations, the times, and the troops involved in each crossing spot.

The plan for crossing the Rhine called for the Ninth Army to spread out along the west side of the river in three corps zones. From north to south, those zones were: XVI Corps, the sector where the Thirtieth and Seventy-Ninth Infantry

ARTISTS OF THE 603RD: ARTHUR SHILSTONE

Arthur Shilstone was seven years old when the stock market crashed in 1929. His father, who worked on Wall Street, was soon out of a job and moved his family from New Jersey to Lake Mahopac in New York State. This move from an urban environment to the country proved to be a turning point for the young artist-to-be. Shilstone discovered a love of hunting and fishing that would remain with him for the rest of his life and guide his artistic career.

A high-school art teacher saw the promise in Shilstone's work and encouraged him to pursue a career in art. Shilstone took his advice and enrolled in Pratt Institute to begin his study of art. However, after a year, he put his education on hold when he was drafted into the army and sent to Fort Meade to become part of the 603rd.

When the war ended, Shilstone returned to New York City and his studies at Pratt. He also took classes at the Brooklyn Museum Art School and the New School for Social Research and completed his degree. He then began his career as an illustrator, beginning at *Life*, one of the country's most popular weekly newsmagazines, known for its photographs and illustrations of the week's events. Shilstone worked on many important stories, including sensational murder trials, funerals of political figures, and an investigation into the sinking of the ocean liner *Andrea Doria* off Massachusetts.

In addition to his work with *Life,* Shilstone also illustrated articles in more than thirty other top magazines, such as *Smithsonian* and *National Geographic.* Later he did a series of paintings for NASA of the space shuttle. His magazine illustrations went "a long way toward defining how Americans have seen historic events" in the time before 24/7 TV news coverage and the Internet.

After thirty years as an illustrator, Arthur Shilstone changed the focus of his art to painting outdoor sporting scenes, becoming "today's premier sporting art watercolorist." His paintings depict scenes across America, including the Alaskan tundra, Chesapeake marshes, and the Adirondack lake country. He illustrated fly-fishing books, as well as annual reports for major U.S. corporations. As one gallery owner said, Arthur Shilstone "manages to paint his riverscapes in such a way that you feel like you've fished that spot."

Shilstone's work hangs in many private collections, as well as in a number of museums, including the American Museum of Fly Fishing and the National Air and Space Museum.

Divisions would cross into Germany at Wesel; XIII Corps, where the Twenty-Third would simulate the Thirtieth and Seventy-Ninth notional divisions and work to convince the Nazis that these divisions would launch their assault from this section of the river on April 1, a week after the real assaults began; and XIX Corps, the southernmost sector on the river that included troops from two infantry divisions, the Twenty-Ninth and Eighty-Third, as well as the Second Armored Division. This section was least affected by the operation. Nevertheless, they were ordered "to keep activity in the front lines as close as possible to that seen in the other two corps sectors."

Operation PLUNDER was commanded by British Field Marshal Montgomery and involved three Allied armies—the U.S. Ninth, the British Second, and the Canadian First—that would cross the Rhine near Wesel, Germany, on the night of March 23–24, north of the Ruhr River. The order of battle called for them to move east after crossing the river before turning to the south. The U.S. First Army would cross to the south—at the area near Cologne, Bonn, and Remagen, Germany—and move east, then north, joining the troops from Wesel in a pincer action that would cut off supplies from the Ruhr Valley that the Nazis needed so desperately.

While the main assault would be at Wesel, the Twenty-Third would play a major role in the success of PLUNDER with its work thirty miles downriver at Düsseldorf. Operation VIERSEN (March 18–April 1, 1945), named after a nearby German city, was the brainchild of Lieutenant Colonel Merrick H. Truly, a liaison officer of the Twenty-Third who was attached to the intelligence section of the Ninth Army.

This operation was part of the Ninth Army's overall deception plan; its objective, as stated in the official report, was "to deceive the enemy as to the actual Rhine River crossing area, strength of the crossing and time of crossing." You may notice the similarity of that objective to the overriding objective of the D-day landing, when the Allies wanted Hitler to believe that the invasion of Europe would be at Pas-de-Calais *after* the real invasion at Normandy.

In this case, the Twenty-Third was to simulate the Thirtieth and Seventy-Ninth Infantry Divisions in XIII Corps. In addition to creating fake divisions in assembly areas in that sector, the Twenty-Third would also advise the army about its cover plan, as well as its techniques, to the commanding general of XIII Corps. After the war, Fox attributed the success of the operation to three "facts": "(1) our role was only part of a giant spectacle involving the whole Ninth Army; (2) we had become veteran deceivers and we used all our tricks; (3) the Nazi [intelligence section] was taken in." To borrow a football metaphor that Fox himself liked to use, the Twenty-Third had created a good game plan and had executed it very well indeed.

Along the Rhine, each of the three corps of the Ninth Army was tasked to "conceal or exaggerate their intentions." The XVI Corps, at the main assault area, prepared for its attack in secrecy. Additional troops entering the area did so at night and did all they could to conceal their movements and true identity. The troops in XIII needed to do the opposite: convince the Germans that it was from their area that the main assault of the Rhine would begin on April 1. This is where the Twenty-Third was to mount its final show. The XIX Corps was farther south on the river where it had given up its artillery to support XVI Corps near Wesel. However, the artillery unit left all their old positions in place and hidden by camouflage.

Because the conflict had become a war of rivers, it had also become a war of bridges. The Nazis had blown up bridges on the Rhine so the Allied troops could not cross into Germany. The Allies were ready to counter that strategy with material to build pontoon and Bailey bridges. In fact, the XXX Corps alone was assigned "8,000 engineers [and was] supplied with 22,000 tons of assault bridging that included 25,000 wooden pontoons."

However, even as the armies were stockpiling bridging material, a group of Americans had crossed one of the few bridges that remained standing over the Rhine. On March 7, about two weeks before PLUNDER would begin, a small group of soldiers from the First Army crossed into Germany. Acting "aggressively, showing extraordinary bravery and initiative," the soldiers under the command of Lieutenant Karl Timmerman raced across the Ludendorff railroad bridge in Remagen, about ninety miles south of Wesel.

The soldiers dug in on the east side of the Rhine and provided cover for the group of engineers that worked hurriedly to cut the cables attached to the German demolition charges on the bridge. The Germans were not about to let the bridge fall into Allied hands. They bombed it, shelled it with artillery, even sent frogmen swimming downriver to blow it up from below. The Nazi attack went on for ten days until the bridge collapsed, "killing twenty-eight engineers and dumping as many as one hundred more into the river." Despite the loss of life, the Americans did lay two pontoon bridges across the river and reinforcements continued to

Allied soldiers crossing the Rhine

pour into Germany, battling their way beyond the bridge-head in a week of "bitter fighting."

Despite the heroism of the men who crossed the bridge at Remagen, the real work of the Rhine crossing was yet to come. Major Ralph Ingersoll, the Special Plans Branch man, wrote that "the big campaign which ended the war was a three-ring circus [with] acts going on simultaneously in all three of the rings." The crossing at Wesel was "Montgomery's show—the much heralded . . . Grand Crossing of the Rhine." The other rings were the First Army in the center and the Third Army in the south. Because of the secret nature of the work of the Twenty-Third, Ingersoll didn't mention that the deception unit was working on a show of its own opposite Düsseldorf.

The Allies assumed that the Germans knew that Montgomery was going to bring Allied forces across the Rhine, although they did not know the time or the place of the main crossing. The Twenty-Third was going to use Monty's reputation as a meticulous planner as part of the deception that would fool the Germans. Operation VIERSEN needed to show that there was no way that the Americans would be ready to attack before April 1. If they could get the Nazis to buy that story, it was reasonable for the Nazis to assume that Montgomery would not risk an earlier crossing if every part of the plan was not exactly as he demanded.

Operation VIERSEN would take all the experience and expertise of the Twenty-Third to execute. It would be the unit's responsibility to simulate the Thirtieth and Seventy-Ninth so that the real infantry divisions could make it to XVI area, where they would be part of the genuine landing force. VIERSEN was "the first time that the Twenty-Third was able to plan for, and use, an entire army for a deception." And the deception unit would use all of its resources— sonic, radio, special effects, camouflage, decoys—in its final operation.

One of the things that the officers and enlisted men of the Twenty-Third had learned in their twenty previous deceptions was that it was often as taxing to plan and execute successful fake operations as it was to plan and execute real operations. And an operation the size of VIERSEN required all the men of the unit to play their parts.

The Twenty-Third was divided into two task forces, each to simulate one of the genuine divisions that would become part of the landing at Wesel. Simenson was in command of the task force that would become the notional Seventy-Ninth

Infantry Division. His unit included about half of the Twenty-Third's resources: sonic, radio, and combat engineers. Lieutenant Colonel Schroeder commanded the other half of the Twenty-Third's resources, plus the Twenty-Third Headquarters Company, in addition to two companies of *camoufleurs.*

The two real infantry divisions totaled about twenty-five thousand men. Imagine the challenge of moving that many troops with their vehicles, artillery, and supplies under the best of conditions. Such an operation was a remarkable feat of planning, logistics, and security, requiring all manner of support, from printing maps and getting them into the hands of the appropriate officers to explaining the route to convoy guides. As with other missions, road signs were put up and fake MPs were stationed to direct the vehicles, check credentials, and make sure no nonmilitary personnel was snooping about.

The real Seventy-Ninth Division, comprising "1,765 vehicles, including 485 artillery vehicles, traveled some sixty miles from Geilenkirchen, Holland, to their staging area on the Rhine." The task facing the Thirtieth Division was even more daunting. That division traveled for more than thirty hours over five days as their convoy moved from Echt, Holland. That division's 3,321 vehicles included "field artillery, combat engineers, camouflage engineers, tank destroyers, armor, antiaircraft artillery, treadway and pontoon bridge companies, maintenance companies, and medical detachments." They always moved at night under radio silence, conditions that increase the risk of road accidents and the possibility of wandering into enemy patrols. Larger convoys were generally broken into smaller units to make

An Allied assault boat crossing the Rhine

their travel less conspicuous. Last, all civilians were cleared from the route the divisions would travel.

As the real divisions made their way slowly from Holland, they passed, as planned, within a few miles of their notional counterparts. From that point, the real divisions peeled off to the north, while the task forces of the Twenty-Third assumed their identities and moved east to their bivouac areas on the west side of the Rhine, about ten miles north of Düsseldorf.

As the Thirtieth and the Seventy-Ninth made their way to the attack sector across the river from Wesel, the Twenty-Third went to work trying to dupe the Germans into believing that the real infantry divisions would try to cross the Rhine near Düsseldorf. The work would be hard and the hours long for all, but the men of the Twenty-Third would show that they were up to the task.

When the Twenty-Third—simulating the Thirtieth and Seventy-Ninth Infantry Divisions—reached their destination near Viersen, Technician Fifth Grade E. Gordon Wilson and his team of three were ordered to München-Gladbach, Germany, to set up their radio command post in "a nice house on an elevation in the middle-class abandoned residential section." Assigned a radio code name and told to acknowledge all messages they received, they were also instructed to transmit only scripted information. Wilson remembered that the team stayed in position "for approximately six days enjoying being in a nice house with comfortable furniture . . . reading the books each of us carried along for those dull moments—and relaxing."

Unlike other earlier, more stressful radio operations, this assignment required only one member of the team to be near the radio and "look up from his reading, pick up the mic, and say 'Roger' and sign off." Since the team was receiving only bogus messages, the signalmen knew what to expect and how they were to respond. And because the messages were fake, meant only for the enemy to overhear, there was nothing for the men to write down and pass along.

The messages told the signalmen (as well as the eavesdropping Germans) that each American unit was checking in to report its position as it moved closer to the area of the simulated buildup. Of course, the messages were not sent from real convoys, but rather from six radio units situated along various roads to their area. And since the transmissions were sent in English, the Germans were to believe that they were hearing a basic traffic control operation.

Wilson believed that the enemy was "glad to have us tell them where our troops were moving to. . . . We were doing them a favor in explaining everything to them" about the movements of the Thirtieth and Seventy-Ninth. Wilson never really worried that the Nazis could track their location and drop in artillery rounds. For one thing, the Germans were receiving a gift of what they considered reliable intelligence about U.S. troop movements. Why silence it? Second, the radiomen in Wilson's team made sure their transmissions lasted only four or five seconds. The Germans, he believed, "just thought we were stupid or so confident of our superiority" that they were sending messages in plain English.

The Germans thinking that they were putting one over on the Americans by eavesdropping on their non-coded transmissions—and, apparently, never giving thought to the possibility that *they* were the ones being played for fools—was the same sort of arrogance they'd shown earlier in the war when they'd refused to periodically (and wisely) change the settings on their Enigma cipher machines when they sent messages about their submarine attack plans. For years, German intelligence believed that Enigma messages were too difficult for the British code breakers at Bletchley Park to crack, when all along the British regularly deciphered most of the Nazi messages.

Of course, radio teams like Wilson's weren't the only members of the Twenty-Third trying to fool the Nazis with spoof radio. Captain Frederic Fox was tasked with creating a "spoof Army Traffic Control net to bring radio attention to XIII Corps by reporting large vehicular movements in that area." As he wrote years after the war, his assignment entailed "wander[ing] around in a jeep pretending to be several convoys of trucks and reporting my progress through powerful radios set up along the way." Like Wilson's team and other similar teams, Fox often sent his messages in English rather than in code "to help the Enemy intercept stations."

A pontoon bridge set up across the Rhine

Such spoof radio transmissions went on day and night, and Fox believed that radio deception was "the key to the whole show." Fox was a stickler for getting things right. The transmissions had to sound "ordinary, dull almost— the hundreds of minor communications between columns of tanks and trucks moving up to assume their places in the assault formations."

In the radio communications, the American signalmen used one of their own quirks to make their transmissions sound authentic. Since Americans were well known for making too much small talk and giving themselves away, the signalmen of the Twenty-Third would do just that, confirming what the Nazi radio interceptor knew about the Americans and their growing presence across the river from Düsseldorf.

Additional rubber dummies were set up in the XIII sector, and a new wrinkle was added to the Twenty-Third's repertoire for this deception: an antiaircraft gun presence that was augmented with sixty-four 40mm and sixteen 90mm rubber guns. The antiaircraft fire would, on some nights, light up the sky with "fierce demonstrations of firepower," that reminded Fox of the opening days of the D-day invasion. But even these "deadly beautiful displays" were merely for show. Since the aerial presence of the Luftwaffe had been so dramatically reduced by Allied air power, its reconnaissance flights were limited.

However, Truly reasoned that substantial antiaircraft barrages would lead the Germans to believe that the Allies were anxious to protect something important in the area, that is, the troops and equipment that would be crossing the Rhine on April 1, the bogus date for the invasion of Germany. The antiaircraft presence was provided by the Nineteenth Anti-Aircraft Artillery Group. However, to strengthen its presence, a notional 90mm battalion position was added, with an array of decoys and dummies.

Yet another new tool in the deception toolbox of VIERSEN was searchlights along the river, creating artificial moonlight by bouncing the strong beams of the searchlights off the low clouds. (Leave it to the deception team to make fake moonlight!) That deflected light provided enough "moonlight" for soldiers to patrol and work on their dummies and flash devices. Of course, it also had the obvious benefit of blinding the Nazi troops across the Rhine and illuminating anything floating in the water. As with other aspects of the deception operation in all three corps sectors, standard practice called for searchlights to be used all along the river and not just where the Twenty-Third's troops and engineers assisting them were simulating the Thirtieth and Seventy-Ninth divisions.

The men might spend their night inflating dummies and moving them into position, but they were not allowed to sleep much during the day. They had their "day jobs" to fulfill, be it as tanker or engineer, *camoufleur* or sonic specialist. They may have needed to be part of a special effects detail, bumping along in the backs of trucks to local villages, giving any ground agents intelligence about the new convoy of troops. And, much to their disdain, there was always guard duty.

Simenson tried his best to make sure that the inflatable decoys and camouflaged positions were in the center of any field or farmyard formation, with genuine vehicles and field guns around the perimeter. Further, the decoys were moved every day so they didn't look too static. He also made sure that the fake tanks were never placed next to real ones where the difference between the two was more likely to be noticed. In some areas along the front, particularly to the north, the dummies were occasionally hit by flying chunks of shrapnel and needed to be repaired. The men who tended to the dummies "always carried chewing gum for quick fixes."

The men in the "sonic cars" were put to work blaring sound effects to fool the Germans. The sonic team relied on its vast library of high-quality sounds to fit a specific tactical situation. The half-tracks "rode solidly, the rear tracks gripping the muddy lanes—four fast tons of bulletproof chassis and armor. Bulletproof, but not tank proof. Not artillery proof." Each sonic car carried a crew of three: a driver, a soldier who did double duty as gunner and radio operator, and the sonic operator. When the covering over the rear of the half-track was peeled back, six 40-watt speakers were ready to blast sound effects to the surrounding area.

Near Anrath, a few miles north of Viersen, the sonic crew in Simenson's task force played four consecutive nights from 7:30 until midnight. Four and a half hours of the sounds of trucks and truck convoys played to alert the nearby villagers that the American Thirtieth and Seventy-Ninth Infantry Divisions were arriving. Only, of course, they weren't. The only Americans in the area were those in Simenson's task force.

During the day, the program was different. Instead of playing the sounds of convoys of large trucks, the sonic men changed to playing sounds of lots of men settling in to their new surroundings, featuring construction sounds: bulldozers and jackhammers, power saws cutting lumber, hammers driving nails. And lots of loud engines from construction equipment. After dark, the sound of a gasoline generator shattered the stillness of the night, "always the heart-stopping moment" for the sonic operators. When the operator uncovered the huge speakers and hit the start switch, "the generator roared alive," sounding like "the loudest motor in the world." With the generator running, the operator began playing the first spool of the wire recording. Slowly, he turned up the volume, and the sounds blasted into the darkness. "Heavy-duty motors groaned, tailgates slammed, soldiers cursed, sergeants barked orders, more trucks arrived," followed by "the noise of a whole fleet of trucks and several hundred men unloading ammunition and supplies."

There was no mistaking what a Nazi ground agent thought he heard. In fact, he would report what he *knew* he heard, a large force of Allied soldiers preparing for an assault. He was sure of it. Except, of course, the preparation he heard was all fake. The men of the Twenty-Third heard something different. All the sounds they played were, the men understood, "the sounds of a target." It is remarkable that the Twenty-Third suffered so few casualties through twenty-one operations.

Special effects were once again a part of the deception operation in the XIII Corps sector. The men wore shoulder patches for the units they were portraying. In addition, more than two hundred directional and informational signs were posted in the surrounding area. Army jeeps led the way to notional supply and water points. Bogus MPs looked authentic, acted with authority, all with a division insignia and "MP" painted on their helmets. Men pretending to be members of the Seventy-Ninth Infantry Division were encouraged to hang their freshly washed laundry outside to dry where any passerby could spot it. And Schroeder ordered similar special effects be played out by his men, including sending a half-track from each company every couple of hours from early morning to early evening to half a dozen surrounding towns and villages.

Even the best deception plans could be easily compromised without tight security. Since ground agents were adept at reading shoulder patches and vehicle bumper markings, directional road signs and convoy traffic, the Allies considered all civilians, including women and children, to be potential Nazi agents. True, the Allies often allowed civilians to gather certain misinformation to pass on to their handlers. However, they also needed to minimize enemy intelligence gathering. So it was that all civilians were often cleared from an area in which the Twenty-Third used dummies or a sonic program. Lieutenant Dick Syracuse, of the 3132nd, and his security platoon protected the sonic cars, while Captain George Rebh and his combat engineers patrolled the surrounding area.

While the real Thirtieth Infantry Division and the Seventy-Ninth Infantry Division counted the days until they crossed the Rhine at Wesel, the men of the Twenty-Third knew nothing beyond what they were ordered to do. Their commanding officers only told them what they needed to know to do their jobs. As Bill Blass later said of the men in his unit, "We had no idea of the Big Picture," even as the Allies were ready to begin the final drive to end the war. It was a standard security measure to tell the men little of how their work fit into the larger battlefield strategy. If the men knew no critical information, they could not divulge it to the enemy if they were captured and interrogated.

The main attack across the Rhine began with an artillery bombardment on March 22 as the British assembled 3,411 artillery pieces and the Americans 2,070 pieces. No wonder the ground shook as the shells thundered home. On the following night, eighty thousand British and Canadian troops landed on the east bank of the river. They were supported by twenty-two thousand airborne paratroopers who had been dropped just behind enemy lines. Wave after wave of Allied troops crossed the Rhine until the last division, the Seventy-Ninth Infantry Division, crossed at three a.m. The final obstacle to Allied victory had been removed. The crossing at Wesel took the Nazis completely by surprise. The Thirtieth and Seventy-Ninth Infantry Divisions met only isolated resistance and suffered thirty-one killed, a remarkably low number of casualties for such a massive attack.

When British prime minister Winston Churchill showed

up on the banks of the Rhine on the morning of March 24, Eisenhower wasn't surprised. Eisenhower noted how Churchill "always seemed to find it possible to be near the scene of action when any particularly important operation was to be launched." As the assault unfolded, Churchill "exclaimed over and over, 'My dear General, the German is whipped. We've got him. He is all through.'" Eisenhower conceded that the prime minister was "merely voicing what all of us felt and were telling each other."

Eisenhower was pleased that the preparations for the attack were so carefully and thoroughly made. Nevertheless, he believed without a doubt that "we owed much to Hitler. There is no question that his General Staff, had it possessed a free hand in the field of military operations, would have

Allied commanders crossing the Rhine on a Bailey bridge

COMMENDATION FOR
THE VIERSEN DECEPTION

HEADQUARTERS
NINTH UNITED STATES ARMY
Office of the Commanding General

APO
29 March 1945

SUBJECT: Commendation

TO: Commanding Officer, 23d Headquarters Special Troops,
Twelfth Army Group.
THRU: Commanding General, Twelfth Army Group

1.   23d Headquarters Special Troops, Twelfth Army Group, was attached to NINTH UNITED STATES ARMY on 15 March 1945 to participate in the operation to cross the RHINE river.

2.   The unit was engaged in a special project, which was an important part of the operation. The careful planning, minute attention to detail, and diligent execution of the tasks to be accomplished by the personnel of the organization reflect great credit on this unit.

3.   I desire to commend the officers and men of the 23d Headquarters Special Troops, Twelfth Army Group, for their fine work and to express my appreciation for a job well done.

W. H. Simpson

W. H. SIMPSON,
Lieutenant General, U.S. Army,
Commanding.

A facsimile of a letter of commendation praising the work of the Twenty-Third for their part in the Rhine crossing foreseen certain disaster on the western bank and would have pulled back the defending forces." But a disaster it was, up and down the Rhine.

As the ground shook with the aerial bombardment and the artillery attack, the Twenty-Third, as planned, began to shut down its operation, removing all signs of the infantry divisions that they had simulated.

The Twenty-Third Headquarters Special Troops had saved their best efforts for their final operation. Operation VIERSEN was "their finest hour," as one historian noted. As Allied troops poured across the Rhine, the trucks for this secret army rumbled off into the night, taking the men of the Twenty-Third and the tricks of their deception trade back to home base for the final time.

EPILOGUE

And so, with the suddenness of a curtain falling at the end a play, the battles were over for the men of the Twenty-Third. They would be involved in no more deception operations. While the Allied armies moved west toward Berlin—"too fast for there to be a front line anymore"—the men of the Twenty-Third "would only have been in the way." Fox's "traveling road show" would perform no more. Troops would continue to fight and die for another six weeks, until the Allies accepted the unconditional surrender of the German forces on May 7, but it was fighting that required no deception.

The Twenty-Third was "immediately split to the four winds and given some very strange assignments." Certainly, assignments that were mostly unrelated to the work the men had done since they landed at Normandy nine months earlier. Part of the Signal Company Special went to the First Army as a radio monitoring unit for the corps and nearly reached the Czechoslovakian border. A wire platoon was tasked with recovering eight hundred miles of the five-hundred-dollars-per-foot "spiral-4" communication wire. Another group from the Signal Company Special worked in the Twelfth Army code room. In fact, these men happened to be on duty in the code room when General Eisenhower announced the surrender of Germany. The rest of the Twenty-Third wound up with the XIII Corps and was assigned to manage the first camps for displaced persons in the Saar-Palatinate region of Germany, not far from their former home base in Luxembourg City.

The displaced persons numbered in the millions at the close of the war, "refugees from the fighting, prisoners of war, slave laborers, and even former Nazis attempting to flee from their past." Making the assignment much more challenging was the fact that there were people of twenty-six nationalities in the camps, setting the stage for dangerous, often deadly confrontations. The Poles and Russians hated each other. And most of the DPs hated and feared the Germans.

The assignment began on April 11 when the men of the Twenty-Third were given command of five camps, in Baumholder, Trier, Bitburg, Wittlich, and Labach. The camps were teeming with one hundred thousand "hungry, homeless, haunted Europeans [who] needed food, shelter, clothes, baths, orientation and transport back to their native lands [and] had to be organized, screened and counted." Despite the complexity of the assignment, the troops brought to it the same dedication they had brought to their deception work. They tamed a mountain of paperwork in several languages and dealt with constant food shortages. Perhaps their greatest accomplishment was the work they did to prevent the spread of typhus in their camps by chemically delousing as many people as they could.

As the men of the Twenty-Third dealt with all the conflicts and dangers in their DP camps, they couldn't help but wonder what would happen to them next. One of the most persistent, and troubling, rumors was that they would return home only to ship out to the Pacific to fight against the Japanese. Bill Blass was one of the men who felt that the Twenty-Third could not duplicate its success against the Japanese. Blass and others in the unit felt that "there was something about the Japanese character . . . that would make it far more difficult" to fool them as they had the Germans. They believed the Japanese "would figure things out quickly."

The soldiers of the Twenty-Third were relieved of the DP camp-management duty on April 28. Nevertheless, they remained in the area, waiting for the telegram from the War Department that would bring the news that they were going home. A month later the telegram arrived. The men of the Twenty-Third were to prepare to return to the United States. Even as they reveled in the good news, the prospect of going to fight the war in the Pacific weighed heavily on their minds.

Sergeant Stanley Wright of the 603rd Engineer Camouflage Battalion probably spoke for many of the men in his unit when he wrote in a letter to his mother, "Back home I can imagine the joy, the celebrating, the enthusiasm—but to most of the boys over here [it was] a moment to relax, an unbelievable calm with a chance to let the mind slip back a year or so and wonder if it was all a dream—[or] nightmare."

The men eagerly began to prepare for "overseas movement," and the big day finally arrived. The convoy left Idar-Oberstein, Germany, for a staging area near Rouen, France. The 350-mile drive took three days through the late spring countryside. To the troops of the Twenty-Third, "dizzy with thoughts of home, every field could have been a rippling flag—or the neon lights of Broadway, a colorful county fair, a Mardi Gras, or a whirling rodeo in Flagstaff, Arizona." The men were going home.

The truck convoy rolled into Camp Twenty Grand on June 16. The following week, they were boarding the *General O. H. Ernst*. The ship was packed as it steamed out of the harbor at Le Havre, France, on June 23. For the journey home, the ship sailed alone with lights, no longer needing to cross the Atlantic in a convoy with a navy escort. Fox recalled that "the voyage was smooth, the quarters clean, the food good, the prospect glorious."

The crossing to the United States was uneventful. The men disembarked at Newport News, Virginia, on July 2, and were taken to Camp Patrick Henry, which reminded Fox of a "gigantic telephone booth," with soldiers lined up for hours waiting to use the phones to call their loved ones.

There were squeals and tears of joy when the men of the Twenty-Third told their families that they were on their way home for a thirty-day leave, or in army-speak, "temporary duty for recuperation, rehabilitation and recovery." The soldiers didn't care what official name the army gave to their leave, as long as they were going home. The men left Camp Patrick Henry with the hope that the war in the Pacific would end before they could be shipped off to fight again.

No doubt the month of "recuperation, relaxation and recovery" passed very quickly for the men, but before they could report to Oakland, California, to prepare for shipping out, the war ended with a brutal finality when the United States dropped an atomic bomb on Hiroshima on August 6 and on Nagasaki three days later, killing nearly two hundred thousand civilians. On August 14, Japan surrendered, effectively ending World War II. Some of the members of the Twenty-Third were already in Oakland, while others were on the way when they received the news. We can only imagine the relief the men felt, knowing they would fight no more. The men were soon assured they would be deactivated by the middle of September.

And so it was that the men of the Twenty-Third ended their service to their country. There was no fanfare for them, "no parades, no ceremonies." The Special Troops "slipped away from the army and vanished from history." The men were ordered to say nothing of their exploits and accomplishments for fifty years. And "like good soldiers, that's exactly what they did," keeping their secrets from family and friends.

Some of them went on to accomplish great things in art, design, and photography. Others had successful careers in business and industry. Still others lived quiet lives in their communities. Regardless of where they went or what they did, the men of the Twenty-Third Headquarters Special Troops forever shared a bond of wartime bravery and secrets.

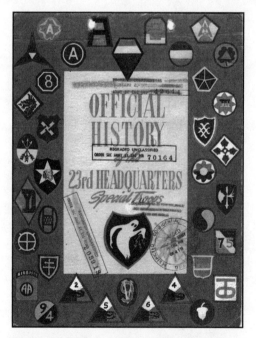

The cover of Fox's "Official History of the 23rd Headquarters Special Troops," which remained classified for fifty years

SOURCE NOTES

INTRODUCTION

p. 1: "the most popular . . . of the officers": Kneece, p. 49.

p. 1: "tall, muscular man with a flamboyant manner": Gerard, p. 49.

p. 2: "shadowy forms . . . emerging from the tree line": ibid., p. 52.

p. 2: "Suddenly my ears . . . to see something?": ibid.

p. 3: "more theatrical than . . . traveling road show": quoted in Beyer, "Freddy Fox Goes to War."

CHAPTER 1: THE GHOST ARMY IS BORN

p. 6: "super secret battalion . . . our antagonists' decisions": quoted in Beyer and Sayles, *Ghost Army,* p. 17.

p. 6: "my con artists": ibid.

pp. 6–7: "reputation for exaggerating his accomplishments" and "certainly didn't . . . on his own": ibid.

p. 7: "capable of simulating . . . appropriate radio communications": quoted in Gawne, p. 17.

p. 7: "Lots of people . . . of the memo": quoted in Beyer, pp. 19–20.

p. 8: "All my life, I had . . . do with ships": Fairbanks, *Salad Days,* p. 374.

p. 8: "next to nothing . . . anxious to learn": ibid., p. 375.

p. 8: "some relatively easy-to-get commissions in the Army": ibid.

p. 9: "of service in any capacity": ibid., p. 381.

p. 9: "further develop cultural relations": ibid., p. 383.

p. 9: "meet and exchange . . . and film people": ibid.

p. 9: "nearly two million . . . come from Germany": ibid., p. 380.

p. 9: "in whatever offhand manner": ibid., p. 383.

p. 9: "most important, I was to find out . . . for our navy": ibid.

p. 9: "nothing but praise" and "I was very pleased . . . 'What next?'": Fairbanks, *Salad Days,* p. 393.

p. 10: "favored land" and "long, bloody and wearisome": Korell.

pp. 10–12: "usually settled in . . . for many generations": Thomas Adam, ed., *Germany and the Americas: Culture, Politics, and History* (Santa Barbara, CA: ABC-CLIO, 2005), p. 28.

p. 12: "secretly ordered diplomats . . . out of Europe": Christopher Klein, "History Stories: How South America Became a Nazi Haven," History Channel website, November 12, 2015, http://www.history.com/news /how-south-america-became-a-nazi-haven.

p. 12: "an estimated nine thousand . . . Nazi war machine": Allan Hall, "Secret Files Reveal 9,000 Nazi War Criminals Fled to South America after WWII," *Daily Mail,* March 19, 2012, http://www.dailymail.co.uk/news /article-2117093/Secret-files-reveal-9-000-Nazi-war-criminals-fled-South -America-WWII.html.

p. 13: "inaccuracies in the paperwork": ibid.

p. 13: "rectification of the . . . were widely unknown": Korell.

p. 14: "to give the enemy . . . an armored group": Fairbanks, *Hell of a War,* p. 148.

p. 14 "even more secret base": ibid.

p. 15: "actual experiments with . . . were carried out": ibid., p. 152.

p. 15: "avid disciple of deception": Gerard, p. 20.

p. 15: "pyramid of deception": ibid., p 21.

p. 15: "cover and deception agency": ibid., p 20.

p. 15: "new, elite, amphibious combat unit": ibid., p. 21.

p. 15: "anything more than . . . wasteful silly tricks": Fairbanks, *Hell of a War,* p. 171.

p. 16: "play a major role in the war": Gawne, p. 75.

pp. 16–17: "tough jobs not . . . a trouble-shooter": quoted in Gerard, p. 40.

p. 18: "seasoned combat veteran . . . recruits into shape" and "volunteers for potentially . . . divulged in advance": Fairbanks, *Hell of a War,* p. 172.

p. 18: four basic requirements: Gerard, p. 25.

p. 19: 180 officers and 300 enlisted men: Gerard, p. 25.

p. 19: "lightly armed plywood . . . of the time": Martin Hill, "Beach Jumpers: Actor Douglas Fairbanks, Jr., and the U.S. Navy's Masters of Deception," *Decoded Past,* September 5, 2013, http://decodedpast.com /beach-jumpers-actor-douglas-fairbanks-jr-and-the-u-s-navys-masters-of -deception/1311.

p. 19: "accomplished complete surprise . . . the German commanders": "The Inception," US Navy Beach Jumpers Association website, http:// www.beachjumpers.com/History/theinception.htm.

p. 20: "were instead planning a 'leapfrog assault' against Genoa": Dwyer, p. 65.

p. 20: "the onset of a new operation": ibid.

p. 21: "We poured out . . . during the invasion": Bob Rainie, "Navy Beach Jumpers, the 1940s," US Navy Beach Jumpers Association website, http:// www.beachjumpers.com/History/1940sBR.htm.

p. 21: "scare the be-jesus out of the enemy" and "BJ factor": quoted in Dwyer, p. 16.

p. 23: "could blow out matches": quoted in Gerard, p. 28.

p. 23: "there might clearly . . . in amphibious operations": Holt, p. 349.

CHAPTER 2: RECRUITMENT AND TRAINING

p. 26: "sneaky and weird": quoted in Kneece, p. 45.

p. 26: "nimble brain . . . what he heard": Gerard, p. 83.

p. 26: "always kind of *harrumph*!": ibid., p. 206.

p. 26: "one of the prime molders": Kneece, p. 35.

p. 28: "the smart guy . . . somebody else's idea": Gerard, p. 87.

p. 28: "the role of scriptwriter and director" and "Behind every operation . . . Fred Fox": Beyer, "Freddy Fox."

p. 28: "just how hard . . . and ease off": Gerard, p. 87.

p. 29: "a wild array of all kinds of people": quoted in Beyer and Sayles, *Ghost Army,* p. 33.

p. 29: "looked on as kind of nutcases . . . and didn't sketch": ibid., p. 34.

p. 29: "single biggest college . . . the nation's history": Louis E. Keefer,

"The Army Specialized Training Program in World War II," Pierce Evans website, http://www.pierce-evans.org/ASTP%20in%20WWII.htm.

p. 29: more than two hundred thousand soldiers to more than two hundred colleges: "ASTP at OSC—Description of the Nationwide ASTP," 89th Infantry Division of World War II website, http://www.89infdivww2.org /memories/astposc2.htm.

p. 30: "every road and . . . on the Potomac": quoted in Arnett.

p. 31: "lots of marching . . . 1903 Springfield rifles": Gerard, p. 67.

p. 31: "swinging on ropes . . . over their heads": ibid.

p. 32: The two main . . . three hundred acres: "Area Allocations, January 1957 for Martin Plant," p. 1, Martin Aviation Archive, via e-mail from Stat Piet, Martin Aviation Archive director, to author, October 3, 2015.

p. 32: the largest aircraft . . . World War II: Richard Clinch in Hannah Cho and Gus Sentementes, "Lockheed to End Manufacturing in Middle River," *Baltimore Sun,* November 18, 2010, http://articles.baltimoresun. com/2010-11-18/business/bs-bz-lockheed-martin-layoffs-20101118_1 _middle-river-thaad-economic-development-director.

p. 32: workforce of fifty-three thousand: ibid.

p. 32: "one of the . . . art of camouflage": Walter Arnett quoted in Arnett.

p. 33: "all the tires . . . crushed in": ibid.

pp. 33–34: "It wasn't as if . . . always down time" and "I just developed . . . ever left me": quoted in Beyer and Sayles, *Ghost Army,* p. 33.

p. 35: "inflatable tanks or the sound guys" and "a stage on which . . . provided that stage": ibid., p. 44.

p. 35: "as much as . . . from radio intercepts": ibid.

p. 36: "ruthless in weeding . . . placed on the men" and "roughly 40 percent . . . to other units": Gawne, p. 29.

p. 39: Would he rather . . . to radio communications?, "Radio—I guess," and "the Good Lord . . . in that decision": Wilson, p. 12.

p. 39: "fairly routine, more like school" and "breeze": ibid., p. 13.

p. 40: "We were all 'shanghaied' . . . top secret.": ibid., p. 14.

p. 40: "the best company of that battalion": Gawne, p. 28.

p. 40: "the only real soldiers": quoted in Beyer, p. 45.

p. 41: "unleash a tremendous . . . around the position": Tony Smejek, "History of Corps of Engineers," Bright Hub Engineering website, updated June 30, 2011, http://www.brighthubengineering.com /structural-engineering/120649-history-of-corps-of-engineers/.

p. 42: "You are an engineer . . . an engineer" and "to be trained . . . for your country": United States War Department, *Basic Field Manual: Engineer Soldier's Handbook, June 2, 1943*, p. 1, University of North Texas Digital Library, https://digital.library.unt.edu/ark:/67531/metadc28313/#who.

pp. 42–44: "played a significant role in the Revolutionary War": "The Corps of Engineers."

p. 44: "ushered in modern . . . observation and mapping": ibid.

p. 46: "soon the command . . . 'heat 'em up'": Gawne, p. 64.

pp. 46–47: "brilliant and eccentric": Gerard, p. 32.

p. 48: "a phantom sound, a sonic illusion" and "lingered in . . . the two speakers": ibid., p. 106.

p. 49: "electronics geek": Christopher Cox, "Edison's Warriors," *Cabinet,* issue 13, (Spring 2004), http://www.cabinetmagazine.org/issues/13 /cox.php.

p. 50: "collective sound of . . . a high level": Gerard, p. 106.

p. 51: "under optimum conditions . . . water at night": ibid., p. 115.

p. 51: "rarely try to project . . . three and a half miles": ibid.

p. 52: "No image of . . . M3 Half-Track vehicle": "Half-Track Personnel Carrier M3 Multi-Purpose Armored Personal Carrier."

p. 52: "in the face . . . and air-burst shells": "Half Track Car M3," *Tank Encyclopedia,* November 28, 2014, http://www.tanks-encyclopedia.com /ww2/US/M3_Halftrack.php.

p. 53: "one-time ax-swinging Maine woodsman" and "the 'why' of . . . cutting and hauling logs": Harrington.

p. 53: "endless chain drives . . . wood or iron": Moore.

p. 53: "generally credited with . . . ahead of him": ibid.

p. 53: could pull up to three hundred tons of logs: ibid.

p. 53: "exactly four years . . . crawler in California": ibid.

pp. 53–54: "Hundreds of thousands . . . see the event": ibid.

p. 54: "the new machine . . . the lumber industry": Harrington.

p. 54: "basic half-track concept . . . World War I": "Half-Track Personnel Carrier M3."

p. 54: "intended for use . . . or personnel carriers": "Halftracks," Olive-Drab website, http://olive-drab.com/od_mvg_vehicle_id_halftrack.php.

p. 54: "the forerunner of . . . World War II": "Half Track Car M2," *Tank Encyclopedia,* January 12, 2016, http://www.tanks-encyclopedia.com /ww2/US/M2_Halftrack.php.

p. 55: "Under the floor . . . would be left": Gerard, p. 112.

CHAPTER 3: SHIPPING OUT . . . AND MORE WAITING

p. 57: "the usual. . . passes to New York": Fox, "Official History," p. 4.

p. 57: "always in a battle . . . foreign diseases": Wilson, p. 17.

p. 57: "canvas-enclosed beds . . . canvas-enclosed walkway": quoted in Arnett.

p. 58: "the largest convoy ever to cross": ibid.

p. 58: "a good clean . . . and rode well": Fox, "Official History," p. 4.

pp. 58–63: "were stacked comfortably like sardines": ibid.

p. 59: In the early . . . by the U-boats: "Ships Hit By U-Boats in WWII: Ship Losses by Month."

p. 59: "without the safe . . . continue the war": Barratt.

p. 59: "created out of desperation": Matthew Hill, "Convoy System: Definition, WW1 & WW2," Study.com, http://study.com/academy/lesson /convoy-system-definition-ww1-ww2.html.

p. 60: "100 or more . . . similar number returning": Gwatkin-Williams.

p. 60: timed as exactly as an express train": ibid.

p. 60: "the more dangerous home waters": ibid.

p. 60: "evasive course plotted . . . of avoiding interception": Barratt.

p. 61: "almost hopeless to . . . the ships would be": Gwatkin-Williams.

p. 62: In 1942, 1,322 ships . . . victimized by U-boats: "Ships Hit By U-Boats in WWII: Ship Losses by Month."

p. 63: "four thousand soldiers . . . airless lower decks": Gerard, p. 122.

p. 63: "if the Germans . . . over our heads!": Arnett.

p. 63: "got sick as a dog": Wilson, p. 17.

p. 63: "If I wasn't . . . made me sick": ibid.

pp. 63–64: "where the meals . . . lose your appetite": ibid.

p. 64: "'You can bet . . . small, close bunks": ibid.

p. 64: "salvation": ibid.

p. 64: "the cooks were friendly . . . last all day" and "almost a pleasure cruise": ibid., p. 18.

p. 64: "figure studies of . . . passing around them": Gerard, p. 123.

p. 64: "Wherever we go . . . be an artist": ibid.

p. 65: "produced in thousands . . . thirty-two states": "Vessel Type EC2: The Liberty Ship," Skylighters: The Story of the 225th AAA Searchlight Battalion from Omaha Beach to V-E Day, http://www.skylighters.org /troopships/libertyships.html.

pp. 65–66: "between 38 and 62 civilian . . . communications equipment": "Reading 1: Liberty Ships," Teaching with Historic Places Lesson Plans, *Liberty Ships and Victory Ships, America's Lifeline in War,* National Park Service, https://www.nps.gov/nr/twhp/wwwlps/lessons/116liberty _victory_ships/116facts1.htm.

p. 66: "the galley and . . . heating were poor": Chester Wardlow, *The Technical Services: The Transportation Corps: Movements, Training, and Supply* (Washington, D.C.: Center of Military History), pp. 145–146.

p. 66: "crude": Lee, p. 12.

p. 66: "these barely livable . . . to over capacity": ibid.

p. 68: "the Castle" and "Moldy Manor'": Gerard, p. 125.

p. 69: "cloak and dagger fashion": Walter Arnett quoted in Arnett.

p. 70: "probably [used] a fake name": ibid.

p. 70: "had it pretty easy": Wilson, p. 20.

p. 70: "you don't go . . . a secret organization": ibid.

p. 71: "clamored for hard . . . salty. Kid food": Gerard, p. 129.

p. 71: "I'll never forget . . . board a ship": Wilson, p. 22.

pp. 71–72: "weighed more than . . . matter of minutes": Gerard, p. 133.

p. 78: "a phantom but static . . . their home ground": ibid., p. 130.

p. 78: "flat dummy Spitfire . . . from the air": Kneece, p. 70.

p. 78: "complete with chimneys . . . painted on metal": ibid.

p. 78: "it was hard . . . could be compared": ibid.

p. 80: "carefully packed in . . . replica it held": Gawne, p. 37.

p. 80: "stretched over air-filled . . . shape and rigidity": Gerard, p. 133.

p. 82: "no after-action reports" and "appear to have . . . for the troops": Gawne, p. 38.

p. 83: "enjoyed the diversions . . . with their equipment": Gerard, p. 135.

p. 84: "first mission . . . Twenty-Third control": Gawne, p. 40.

p. 84: "an area where. . . be very weak," ibid.

p. 85: "Allied ships twice . . . an air alert": ibid., p. 43.

CHAPTER 4: THE TWENTY-THIRD GETS INTO ACTION

p. 87: "officially called RESIDUE or informally, 'Garbage'": Fox, "Official History," p. 7.

p. 88: "no one cared . . . the weather, perfect": ibid., pp. 6–7.

p. 88: "more curious than frightful": ibid., p. 7.

p. 91: "remained wedged within . . . twenty miles deep": Atkinson.

p. 91: "intense, grim, and . . . a few yards": ibid.

p. 91: "carried everywhere for nearly two years": Gerard, p. 146.

p. 91: "to keep from . . . writing or talking": ibid.

p. 92: "oldest collegiate musical-comedy . . . in the nation": "Ghost Army Veterans: Fred Fox," *The Ghost Army of World War II* website, http://www.ghostarmy.org/bio/f/Ghost_Army_Veterans/286.

p. 92: "to great acclaim": Beyer, "Freddy Fox Goes to War."

p. 92: "looked like a . . . professor of English": Gerard, p. 87.

p. 92: "passionately" and "a more theatrical approach to their deceptions": Beyer and Sayles, *Ghost Army*, p. 83.

p. 94: "simultaneously dazzled by . . . field and village": ibid., pp. 148–149.

p. 96: "as he slowly . . . boom-boom—ha ha!": Gawne, p. 51.

pp. 98–99: "One third of . . . poor camouflage jobs": ibid., p. 53.

p. 99: "There is every . . . good was done": Fox, "Official History," p. 8.

p. 99: "considerable help": ibid.

p. 100: "appears to have been . . . with the contents": Gawne, pp. 57–58.

p. 100: "The attitude of . . . AND ARMY PROCEDURE": ibid., 58.

p. 100: "failure to play its role thoroughly": ibid.

p. 100: "servile obedience": ibid.

p. 100: "lack of appreciation . . . of the theater": ibid.

p. 100: "just as much . . . the field artillery": ibid.

p. 101: "equally essential to . . . be among them": ibid., p. 59. [quote not confirmed]

p. 101: "all you got . . . go to sleep" and "forgot that we were in show business": ibid.

p. 101: "merely represent the . . . typical GI fashion": ibid.

p. 101: "with its scarlet license plate is essential": ibid.

p. 101: "Is not the . . . contrary to ARs?": ibid.

p. 101: "tactical dispositions and . . . of fighting units": ibid., p. 60.

p. 102: "theater attitude": ibid.

p. 102: "its needs, capabilities . . . of the Army": Fox, "Official History," p. 8.

p. 102: "DECEPTION 'salesmen'—selling . . . whomever would listen": ibid.

p. 103: "mainly geographical": Fox, "Deception Team," p. 11.

p. 103: "first time the Twenty-Third . . . in the area": Gawne, p. 86.

pp. 103–104: "We sent four . . . over the place": quoted in Gerard, p. 162.

p. 104: "It was a wild . . . was confused": Fox, "Deception Team," p. 10.

p. 105: "quietly told . . . the right direction": Gawne, p. 90.

p. 105: "transformed into a . . . removed bumper covers": ibid., p. 92.

p. 107: "Normally there is . . . number of reasons": ibid., p. 95.

p. 108: "seemed to be responsible for all of my paintings": ibid.

p. 108: "trained his eyes . . . rather than lines": Nancy Mattoon, "Wartime Artists Learn the Art of War," *Booktryst* (blog), March 15, 2010, http://www.booktryst.com/2010/04/wartime-artists-learn-art-of-war.html.

p. 108: "utilize only . . . species of bird": ibid.

p. 108: "we'll find you": quoted in Paltrow.

p. 109: "I decided . . . just for me": quoted in Gerard, p. 64.

p. 109: "training and morale . . . teach and inspire": ibid.

p. 109: "careful observer of . . . in American art": quoted in "President Obama to Award 2012 National Medal of Arts and National Humanities Medal," The White House, Office of the Press Secretary, July 3, 2013, https://www.whitehouse.gov/the-press-office/2013/07/03/president -obama-award-2012-national-medal-arts-and-national-humanities-m.

p. 110: "strewn with the . . . flattened by tanks": Gerard, p. 168.

p. 111: "stunning slaughter and great victory for the Allies," ibid.

p. 111: "continued improvement in the technique of deception" and "a worsening in the employment of it": Fox, "Official History," p. 11.

p. 112: "simple and rather . . . Brest to surrender": Gerard, p. 173.

p. 112: "giving up fairly readily": Fox, "Official History," p. 12.

p. 113: "only leaky pup . . . rest before daylight": Gerard, p. 179.

p. 113: "superb": Fox, "Official History," p. 12.

p. 113: "what was, in . . . American-induced ambush": Kneece, p. 87.

p. 114: "blithely and naively . . . an unmitigated disaster": ibid.

p. 114: "The real tanks . . . let us down!" quoted in Gerard, p. 184.

p. 114: "When I saw . . . It was horrible": quoted in Kneece, p. 87.

p. 115: "absurd, potentially suicidal": Gerard, p. 176.

p. 115: "How we came . . . was absolutely stupid": ibid.

p. 115: "Suddenly the flash . . . with blinding surprise": ibid.

p. 116: "least visible and . . . the most effective": ibid., p. 177.

p. 118: "the normal intervals . . . between companies," and "shifting of gears . . . voices of guides": ibid., p. 178.

p. 118: "the sound effects . . . extremely realistic" and "no distortion": quoted in Gawne, p. 99.

p. 119: "very dedicated . . . force of soldiers": ibid., p. 107.

CHAPTER 5: THE FIRST BIG TEST

p. 122: "surely too wise . . . to their homeland": Persico, p. 9.

p. 122: "literally ran out . . . the German border": ibid.

pp. 122–123: "capture of the . . . a difficult operation": Eisenhower, p. 326.

p. 124: "possibly we could . . . three weeks earlier": ibid., p. 327.

pp. 124–129: "consisted of truncated . . . three to four feet tall": "The Siegfried Line," Lost Images of World War II, http://lostimagesofww2.com /photos/places/siegfried-line.php.

p. 125: "ordinarily required 700–750 . . . about 20,000 tons": Bradley and Blair, p. 320.

p. 125: eight hundred thousand gallons of gas: Colley, "On the Road to Victory: The Red Ball Express."

p. 125: "exclusive use of . . . available motor transport": Ruppenthal, p. 559.

p. 126: "evacuation hospitals, gas . . . ordnance maintenance companies": ibid., p. 570.

p. 126: "African American troops . . . the supply lines rolling": Colley, *The Road to Victory*, p. xv.

p. 126: 75 percent of the supply drivers . . . were African American: Colley, "On the Road to Victory."

p. 126: "the majority of . . . manned by blacks": Colley, *The Road to Victory*, p. xv.

p. 127: "more like a . . . stock car race": Colley, "On the Road to Victory."

p. 128: "I've driven when . . . feel the road": quoted in Albrecht.

p. 128: "falling asleep on . . . know the difference": ibid.

p. 128: "more than six thousand . . . tons of supplies": Colley, *The Road to Victory*, p. xv.

p. 128: "Red Ball Line . . . combat and supply": "Red Ball Express Created," National World War II Museum website, http://www.nww2m.com/2014/08/red-ball-express-created/.

p. 128: "contributed significantly to . . . Army in France": Colley, *The Road to Victory*, pp. xiv.

p. 129: "home by Christmas . . . a possible dream": Persico, p. 9.

p. 130: "unspent sting": ibid.

p. 130: "perhaps the most fortified city in Europe": Gerard, p. 200.

p. 132: "the riskiest ploy . . . had yet dared": ibid.

p. 134: "civilians were observed . . . asking 'friendly questions'": Beyer and Sayles, *Ghost Army*, pp. 117–118.

p. 134: "'atmosphere'—observable, convincing 'evidence of a buildup'": Gerard, p. 201.

p. 135: "loved this part . . . farces and dramas": ibid., p. 199.

p. 135: "like advance men . . . at the fairground": ibid.

p. 135: "barreling through the . . . with machine guns": Fox, "The Deception Team," p. 15.

p. 135: "scouted the high . . . snipers usually hid": Gerard, p. 198.

p. 135: "Nothing gives the . . . High Ranking Brass": Fox, "The Deception Team," p. 15.

p. 135: "middle-aged Princeton alumnus with a military moustache": ibid.

p. 136: "despised looters in any army": Gerard, p. 199.

p. 136: "can tell a lot . . . is being said": Gawne, pp. 113–114.

p. 137: seventy messages: ibid., p. 114.

p. 139: "the sonic deception was considered very effective": ibid., p. 116.

p. 139: "enormous sounds . . . division was amassing": quoted in Beyer and Sayles, *Ghost Army*, p. 116.

p. 139: "put out that goddamned cigarette now": ibid.

p. 139: "jumping on anything . . . out of Luxembourg": quoted in Gerard, p. 202.

p. 139: "That made us feel good": Fox, "The Deception Team," p. 15.

p. 139: "beginning to tell . . . in the dark": quoted in Beyer and Sayles, *Ghost Army,* p. 116.

p. 140: "never had to . . . myself with drawing": ibid., p. 27.

p. 140: "soft-spoken kid with . . . sense of humor": Gerard, p. 55.

p. 140: "Everybody was in the service": ibid., p. 56.

p. 140: "marveled at the . . . sense of movement": ibid., p. 55.

p. 141: "lost arms and . . . together by bandages": ibid., p. 144.

p. 141: "was struck by . . . reality of today": quoted in Beyer and Sayles, p. 63.

p. 141: "there was no . . . bad about that": quoted in Gerard, p. 241.

p. 143: "By this time . . . about the woods!": ibid., p. 202.

p. 143: "joined their shelter . . . dryness and warmth": ibid.

p. 143: "Every time a . . . from the concussion": Wilson, p. 53.

p. 144: "strung tripwires attached . . . their bivouac areas": Gerard, p. 204.

p. 144: "ratcheted up the anxiety level": ibid., p. 203.

p. 145: "did things come . . . as it should": Gawne, p. 119.

p. 145: "our first operation . . . professionally and correctly": quoted in Beyer and Sayles, *Ghost Army,* p. 121.

p. 145: "even the most . . . did not predict": Fox, "Official History," p. 16.

p. 145: "full of atrocious Nazi murals": ibid.

p. 145: "Usually, they are . . . toward bad taste": quoted in Gerard, p. 208.

p. 145: "It began to look . . . for the winter": Fox, "Official History," p. 16.

p. 146: "the huge, clanking . . . in full daylight": ibid., p. 17.

p. 146: "ride with the punch": ibid.

p. 146: "a large step forward": Gawne, p. 121.

p. 147: "to be briefed thoroughly . . . of the nets": Fox, "Official History," p. 17.

p. 148: "fit perfectly with . . . was being portrayed": Gawne, p. 123.

p. 149: "when we left . . . entirely different unit": Wilson, p. 52.

p. 150: "greatly endangered": Fox, "Official History," p. 17.

p. 150: "big lesson re-learned . . . the covered unit": ibid.

p. 151: "as satisfying to . . . not as scary": Fox, "Deception Team," p. 17.

p. 151: "loud, short, and possibly furious": Fox, "Official History," p. 17.

p. 151: "mostly enjoyed Luxembourg": ibid., p. 18.

CHAPTER 6: A TRIO OF DECEPTIONS

p. 153: "overwhelmed with affection . . . lasted for decades": Gerard, p. 211.

p. 153: "I wanted to . . . for so long": quoted in Beyer and Sayles, *Ghost Army,* p. 132.

p. 153: "Four years of . . . you smiling boys": quoted in Gerard, p. 211.

p. 154: "stretched the abilities . . . to the limit": Gawne, p. 137.

p. 154: The operation was . . . dummy artillery pieces: ibid.

p. 154: "real shooting pieces": Fox, "Official History," p. 19.

p. 156: "Squads alternate firing . . . in this weather," quoted in Gerard, p. 217.

p. 156: "Spent horrible night . . . shakes the hut": quoted in Kneece, p. 188.

p. 156: "one man with . . . maintained air pressure": Gawne, p. 141.

p. 156: "packing mud on . . . a normal shape": ibid., p. 144.

p. 157: "a receptacle for . . . fill it up": quoted in Beyer and Sayles, *Ghost Army,* p. 127.

p. 158: "I had to . . . the next morning": quoted in Gerard, p. 210.

p. 158: "scrounged or built . . . in his jeep": ibid., p. 209.

p. 158: "art conscious again . . . a week now": ibid., p. 214.

p. 158: "Bundled up in a shapeless wool suit": ibid., p. 222.

p. 159: "only live USO . . . the Special Troops": ibid., p. 220.

p. 159: This operation involved . . . 431 enlisted men: Gawne, p. 148.

p. 159: "revolved around a . . . of division moves": Fox, "Deception Team," p. 18.

p. 159: "a deathtrap. . . in the open": Gerard, p. 215.

p. 160: "required keen observation . . . from the air": "Arthur Singer," Art of the Stamp, Smithsonian National Postal Museum website, http://postalmuseum.si.edu/artofthestamp/subpage%20table%20images/artwork/Artist%20Bios/arthursinger.htm.

p. 160: "established him as a modern Audubon": Stephanie Strom, "Arthur B. Singer, 72, Artist, Dies; Painted 50 State Birds on Stamps," *New York Times,* April 8, 1990, http://www.nytimes.com/1990/04/08/obituaries/arthur-b-singer-72-artist-dies-painted-50-state-birds-on-stamps.html.

p. 160: "in the first . . . finest bird artists": "Biography," Arthur Singer, http://www.singerarts.com/arthursinger/bio.htm.

p. 161: "is believed to . . . United States postage": Stephanie Strom, "Arthur B. Singer, 72, Artist, Dies; Painted 50 State Birds on Stamps," *New York Times,* April 8, 1990, http://www.nytimes.com/1990/04/08/obituaries/arthur-b-singer-72-artist-dies-painted-50-state-birds-on-stamps.html.

p. 162: "enjoying the drive . . . spread out below": Wilson, p. 56.

p. 162: "small plane": ibid.

p. 162: "a tremendous explosion . . . quarter of a mile": ibid.

p. 162: "one would fly . . . they were doing": ibid., p. 57.

p. 162: "made the windows . . . sputter and stall": Fox, "Deception Team," p. 18.

p. 163: "careful notes . . . water distribution points": Gawne, p. 148.

p. 164: "a fake within a fake": Heckman et al., p. 12.

p. 165: "Patrols third Bn . . . but OK now": quoted in Gawne, pp. 147–148.

p. 165: "some grumbling from . . . ridiculous radio test": ibid., p. 148.

p. 165: "time allowed for . . . encountered so far": ibid., p. 149.

p. 166: "The rest of the play. . . Special Effects Section": Fox, "Deception Team," p. 19.

p. 167: "was definitely not our idea . . . would not call resting": Wilson, p. 57.

p. 167: "keep . . . moving around . . . the German Army": ibid.

p. 168: "all the tricks . . . Special Troops' inventory": Gerard, p. 218.

p. 168: "Throughout history, wars . . . not crossing rivers": Patton, p. 97.

p. 168: "create all the . . . major bridging assault": Gerard, p. 218.

pp. 168–169: The detachment of . . . the sonic company: Gawne, p. 155.

p. 169: "longest Bailey bridge in the world": Gerard, p. 219.

p. 169: "merely splattered the . . . Ninetieth Division atmosphere": Fox, "Official History," p. 19.

p. 170: "one of the three . . . to our victory": quoted in "UK Military Bridging—Equipment (Bailey Bridge)," Think Defence website, January 8, 2012, http://www.thinkdefence.co.uk/2012/01/uk-military-bridging -equipment-the-bailey-bridge/#Building_a_Bailey_Bridge.

p. 170: "could never have . . . of Bailey bridging": ibid.

p. 171: It's been estimated . . . two Bailey bridges a day and "the vast store of them": "How the Army's Amazing Bailey Bridge Is Built," *The War Illustrated* 8, no. 198 (January 19, 1945), p. 564, http:// www.thewarillustrated.info/198/how-the-armys-amazing-bailey-bridge -is-built.asp.

p. 171: One engineering battalion . . . valued engineering assistance: "Bailey Bridge," Skylighters: The Story of the 225th AAA Searchlight Battalion from Omaha Beach to V-E Day, http://www.skylighters.org /encyclopedia/bailey.html.

p. 171: "throw these bridges . . . in a few hours": Sanders.

p. 172: "by a crew . . . crew of 148": ibid.

p. 173: "I have never . . . in my life": Patton, pp. 172–173.

p. 173: "extended for a . . . shoulder to shoulder": ibid., p. 173.

CHAPTER 7: A DEADLY WINTER

p. 175: "led to boredom, obesity": Fox, "Official History," p. 20.

p. 175: "kept busy and . . . first aid and sanitation": ibid.

p. 176: "the dullest part of the Western Front": ibid.

p. 176: "a short course of leisurely combat": Gerard, p. 227.

p. 177: "to split the . . . vicinity of Trier": Gawne, p. 165.

p. 177: "did not handle . . . players and devices": Fox, "Deception Team," p. 21.

p. 177: "proper counterintelligence measures, and safeguards": Gawne, p. 167.

p. 178: "to be a completely. . . Luxembourg that morning": Wilson, p. 63.

p. 178: "usually in the . . . wanted no surprises": Gerard, pp. 227–228.

p. 179: "operating a radio, . . . found the time": Wilson, p. 63.

p. 179: "10 meals for . . . of these boxes": ibid., p. 62.

p. 179: "similar to the . . . soap, towels, etc.": "U.S. Army Field Rations: The 10-in-1 Ration," Modeling the U.S. Army in WWII website, http://www.usarmymodels.com/ARTICLES/Rations/10in1rations.html.

pp. 179–180: "only biscuits, candy . . . during the day": ibid.

p. 180: "to think we did . . . wanted to hide": Wilson, p. 64.

p. 180: "that could be heard . . . equipment actually moving": ibid.

p. 181: "no outsider could . . . the real thing": ibid.

p. 181: "the visible duties . . . divisional engineer battalion": Gawne, p. 173.

p. 181: "particularly helpful in . . . division engineer unit": ibid., p. 174.

p. 182: "very sloppy in their radio traffic": Kneece, p. 221.

pp. 182–183: "didn't have the luxury . . . no moonlight": Wilson, p. 65.

p. 183: "final, desperate blow . . . reserve was thrown": quoted in Kneece, p. 214.

p. 183: "cunning title": Alex Kershaw, *The Longest Winter: The Battle of the Bulge and the Epic Story of WWII's Most Decorated Platoon* (Cambridge, MA: Da Capo, 2004), p. 30.

p. 183: "fierce defense of . . . the Third Reich": ibid.

p. 183: The plan of . . . hundred artillery pieces: "Battle of the Bulge."

p. 184: "all the northern . . . off and destroyed": Stokesbury, p. 352.

p. 185: "disguised raiding parties," "prompt reinforcement," and "an organized attempt . . . in American uniforms": Cole, p. 269.

p. 185: "considerable reputation as a daring commando leader": ibid.

p. 185: "unlimited powers to prepare his mission": Beevor, p. 92.

p. 185: "numbering about two . . . could speak English": Cole, p. 270.

p. 185: "Everything I know . . . punishable by death": quoted in Beevor, p. 92.

p. 186: "to learn the . . . improve their accent": ibid., p. 93.

p. 186: "two hours a . . . down the knife'": ibid.

p. 187: "20 Sherman tanks . . . about 30 jeeps": Hollway.

p. 187: "very young American . . . away at night": ibid.

p. 188: "a great mishmash": Stokesbury, p. 352.

p. 188: "the dullest part of the Western Front": Fox, "Official History," p. 20.

p. 188: "arrival of thousands . . . Twenty-Third units": ibid., p. 22.

p. 188: "ignominiously westward . . . flophouse barracks": ibid.

pp. 188–189: "Organization alerted, documents . . . the entire night": ibid.

p. 189: "the enthusiasm with . . . guns were fired" and "it was the first . . . at the enemy": ibid.

p. 189: "an attempt to . . . order of battle": ibid., p. 23.

p. 189: The twenty-nine signalmen . . . from the 406th: Gawne, p. 181.

p. 190: "The brevity of . . . or the Eightieth": Fox, "Official History," p. 23.

p. 191: "beautiful, clear day . . . bombers flying over": Wilson, p. 71.

p. 191: "as far as we could see to the north of us": ibid.

p. 191: "glittering formations" and "methodically destroy the . . . the slushy mud": Gerard, p. 233.

p. 191: "things were getting . . . they should be": ibid., p. 234.

p. 192: "For the first . . . blown to hell": ibid.

p. 192: "Christmas was a very sad day for everyone": Fox, "Official History," p. 23.

p. 192: "out of anything . . . to get warm": quoted in Gerard, p. 235.

pp. 193–194: "pale and gaunt, many . . . they were wearing": ibid.

p. 194: "refuse of war . . . the slave camps": ibid., p. 236.

p. 194: "rations, candy, crackers . . . against sore throats": ibid.

p. 194: "little package of . . . and small toys": ibid.

p. 194: "did their modest part . . . of kids happy": ibid.

p. 194: "absolutely speechless . . . seen candy before": ibid.

p. 194: "Most of the . . . 'O Holy Night.'": ibid.

pp. 194–195: "a very dirty and windy": Fox, "Official History," p. 23.

pp. 194–195: "depressing city filled . . . it too crowded": ibid.

p. 195: "grinding, bloody nature . . . the Western Front": "Battle of Verdun Begins," History Channel website, http://www.history.com /this-day-in-history/battle-of-verdun-begins.

p. 195: "a bunch of slobs": quoted in Beyer and Sayles, *Ghost Army,* p. 177.

p. 195: "very flamboyant, very outgoing, very cheerful": ibid., p. 176.

p. 195: Tompkins thought enough . . . was in France: Gerard, p. 238.

p. 195: "cover the non-secret . . . the Nazi bulge": Fox, "Official History," p. 23.

p. 195: "small effort by . . . Signal Service Battalion": ibid.

p. 196: "a miserable place to grow up in": quoted in Leila E. B. Hadley, "Man à la Mode," *Saturday Evening Post,* April 6, 1968: 30–31.

p. 196: "captivated by the . . . and fashion magazines": "Bill Blass," Biography.com, http://www.biography.com/people/bill-blass-9215129.

p. 196: "filled the margins . . . of Hollywood-inspired fashions": "Bill Blass," Oral Cancer Foundation, website: http://oralcancerfoundation.org /people/bill_blass.php.

p. 197: "beauty of being . . . your immediate circumstances": ibid.

p. 198: "surrounded by dozens . . . hit the ground": Wilson, p. 70.

p. 198: "as the crowd . . . grabbing for food": ibid.

p. 198: "in the maze . . . item I thought": ibid.

pp. 198–199: "entirely different feeling . . . in our garbage": ibid.

p. 199: "It is hard . . . cold, unlighted barracks": Fox, "Official History," p. 23.

p. 200: "the fabled luck . . . Troops ran out": Gerard, p. 240.

p. 200: "rather sloppy and unsatisfactory": Fox, "Official History," p. 24.

p. 201: "frightfully cold but . . . was snugly billeted": ibid., p. 25.

p. 201: "what they did . . . a river crossing": Gerard, p. 241.

p. 201: "good example of . . . sounds to work": Gawne, p. 205.

p. 202: "one of the . . . [operations] ever attempted": Fox, "Official History," p. 25.

p. 202: "plenty of warm . . . happened to be": ibid.

p. 202: "had come to look . . . I always had": Wilson, p. 79.

p. 202: "dangerous transition": Gerard, p. 243.

p. 203: "degree of success was unknown": Gawne, p. 215.

CHAPTER 8: AFTER THE BATTLE OF THE BULGE

p. 205: "doomed to disappointment . . . still not destroyed": Stokesbury, p. 349.

p. 205: "The beast fought blindly on": ibid.

p. 207: "the picture of . . . and establishing outposts": Gawne, p. 219.

p. 208: "clearly...taken by the ruse": Gerard, p. 248.

p. 208: "adding to the . . . increasing its patrolling": Gawne, p. 219.

p. 209: "said something like . . . look that way": Wilson, p. 81.

p. 209: "still possibly unconvinced": ibid.

p. 210: "was becoming more popular": Fox, "Official History," p. 27.

p. 210: "fairly harmless": ibid.

p. 211: "135 rounds of . . . rounds of artillery": ibid.

p. 211: "the one experience . . . not shoot back": Gerard, p. 249.

pp. 211–212: "can still hear . . . It's indelible": ibid.

p. 212: "quick-thinking response . . . unit to unit": Gawne, p. 223.

p. 213: "talented machinist who . . . Special Troops needed": Gerard, 210.

p. 213: "to subsidize their meager rations": "A Brief History of Trench Art,"

UK Trench Art website, http://www.trenchart.co.uk/History/history01 .html.

p. 213: "first war where . . . could take place": ibid.

p. 213: "with impoverished locals . . . tourists and traders": ibid.

p. 214: "bullets, aluminum, buttons . . . assemblages or souvenirs": "World War II Trench 'Art'ifact," Lynchburg Museum System website, http://www .lynchburgmuseum.org/blog/2013/11/world-war-ii-trench-artifact.html.

p. 215: "Nothing to do . . . if we wanted": Wilson, pp. 82–83.

p. 215: "how close he . . . tailfeathers clipped": ibid., p. 83.

p. 216: "sat around in . . . in the least": ibid., p. 84.

p. 216: "much food, chocolate . . . in our truck": ibid.

p. 216: "left a large pile . . . with the others": ibid., p. 85.

p. 216: "this repaid them . . . family to eat": ibid.

p. 216: "unstable situation": Fox, "Official History," p. 28.

p. 217: "small tailspin": ibid.

p. 217: "one of the shortest operations on record": ibid.

p. 217: "deadliest show they ever staged": Gerard, p. 253.

pp. 217–218: "We were stuck . . . were stuck there": ibid., p. 252.

p. 218: "Fear. Fear. Everything you're doing is fear": ibid., p. 254.

p. 218: "nothing special about . . . typical harassing fire": Gawne, p. 233.

p. 218: "if you just happened . . . of that trip": Wilson, p. 86.

p. 218: "the best way . . . day will bring": ibid., p. 85.

p. 218: "Even in a . . . throat in half": Fox, "The Deception Team," pp. 24–25.

p. 218: "building up vehicular . . . of the Moselle": ibid.

pp. 218–221: "I can think . . . peaceful, generous lives": quoted in Gerard, p. 255.

p. 219: "painted neckties for . . . whatever they wanted": ibid., p. 54.

p. 219: "he could use his sense . . . the war effort": ibid., p. 55.

p. 220: "greatly inspires me . . . with my painting": quoted in Beyer and Sayles, *Ghost Army,* p. 181.

p. 220: "soft time": Gerard, p. 260.

p. 220: "Although I am . . . to the outfit": ibid.

Chapter 9: The Final Deception

p. 223: "with its coal . . . more vital objective": MacDonald, *The Last Offensive,* p. 18.

p. 223: "It is difficult, in . . . as 1945 opened": ibid., p. 8.

p. 224: "shadow of an army": ibid., p. 301.

p. 224: "suspicion to callous resignation": ibid.

p. 224: "failing to blow . . . to the end": quoted in Lippman.

p. 224: "My orders are categorical. Hang on!": ibid.

p. 224: "source of weird . . . a historic moat": MacDonald, *The Last Offensive,* p. 294.

pp. 224–225: "varied from 900 to 1,500 feet": ibid., p. 297.

p. 225: "not only wide but treacherous": Eisenhower, p. 388.

p. 225: "monumental crossing . . . operation since Normandy": Gerard, p. 262.

p. 225: "more than 37,000 . . . in the assault": Lippman.

p. 225: "world-record 66-mile-long smoke screen": ibid.

p. 225: "a half million . . . was just beautiful": Gerard, p. 292.

p. 227: "a long way . . . seen historical events": "Arthur Shilstone."

p. 227: "today's premier sporting art watercolorist": "Arthur Shilstone: A Lifetime of Drawing and Painting," American Museum of Fly Fishing website, http://www.amff.org/product/arthurc-shilstone-a-lifetime-of -drawing-and-painting/.

p. 227: "manages to paint . . . fished that spot": "Arthur Shilstone."

p. 228: "to keep activity . . . corps sectors": Gawne, p. 238.

p. 229: "to deceive the enemy . . . time of crossing": quoted in Fox, "Deception Team," p. 25.

p. 229: "(1) our role was only. . . was taken in": ibid.

p. 229: "conceal or exaggerate their intentions": ibid.

p. 230: "8,000 engineers and . . . 25,000 wooden pontoons": Lippman.

p. 230: "aggressively, showing extraordinary bravery and initiative": "Crossing the Rhine River: March 1945," Globe at War, August 7, 2011, http://www.globeatwar.com/article/crossing-rhine-river-march-1945.

p. 230: "killing twenty-eight engineers . . . into the river": Gerard, p. 264.

p. 231: "bitter fighting": ibid.

p. 231: "the big campaign . . . of the rings" and "Montgomery's show . . . of the Rhine": Ingersoll, p. 297.

p. 232: "the first time . . . for a deception": Gawne, p. 235.

p. 233: "1,765 vehicles, including . . . on the Rhine": Gerard, p. 268.

p. 233: "field artillery, combat . . . and medical detachments": ibid.

p. 235: "a nice house . . . residential section": Wilson, p. 90.

p. 235: "for approximately . . . moments—and relaxing": ibid.

p. 235: "look up from . . . and sign off": ibid.

p. 235: "glad to have . . . everything to them": ibid., p. 91.

p. 236: "just thought we were . . . our superiority": ibid.

p. 236: "spoof Army Traffic . . . in that area": Fox, "Deception Team," p. 27.

p. 236: "wander[ing] around in . . . along the way": ibid.

p. 236: "to help the Enemy intercept stations": ibid.

p. 237: "the key to the whole show": Gerard, p. 276.

p. 237: "ordinary, dull almost . . . the assault formation": ibid.

pp. 237–238: Additional rubber dummies . . . 90mm rubber guns: Fox, "The Deception Team," p. 26.

p. 238: "fierce demonstrations of firepower" and "deadly beautiful displays": ibid.

p. 239: "always carried chewing gum for quick fixes": Gerard, p. 270.

p. 239: "rode solidly, the . . . Not artillery proof": ibid., p. 278.

p. 240: "always the heart-stopping moment": ibid., p. 279.

p. 240: "the generator roared alive" and "the loudest motor in the world": ibid.

p. 240: "Heavy-duty motors groaned . . . more trucks arrived" and "the noise of . . . ammunition and supplies": ibid.

p. 241: "the sounds of a target": ibid.

p. 242: "we had no idea of the Big Picture": ibid., p. 286.

p. 242: The main attack . . . Americans 2,070 pieces: Lippman.

p. 242: They were supported by twenty-two thousand airborne paratroopers: Chen, "Crossing the Rhine."

p. 243: "always seemed . . . to be launched": Eisenhower, p. 390.

p. 243: "exclaimed over and . . . is all through" and "merely voicing what all . . . telling each other": ibid.

pp. 243–245: "We owed much . . . defending forces": ibid., p. 394.

p. 245: "their finest hour": Gerard, p. 289.

EPILOGUE

p. 247: "too fast for . . . line anymore": Gerard, p. 297.

p. 247: "would only have been in the way": Fox, "Official History," p. 32.

p. 247: "traveling road show": Beyer, "Freddy Fox Goes to War."

p. 247: "immediately split to . . . very strange assignments": Fox, "Official History," p. 32.

p. 248: "refugees from the . . . from their past": Gawne, p. 280.

p. 248: "hungry, homeless, haunted . . . screened and counted": Fox, "Official History," p. 32.

pp. 248–249: "there was something . . . far more difficult": Kneece, p. 268.

p. 249: "would figure things out quickly": ibid.

p. 249: "Back home I . . . dream—[or] nightmare": Beyer and Sayles, *Ghost Army,* p. 218.

p. 249: "dizzy with thoughts . . . in Flagstaff, Arizona": Fox, "Official History," p. 33.

p. 250: "the voyage was . . . the prospect glorious": ibid.

p. 250: "gigantic telephone booth": ibid., p. 35.

p. 250: "temporary duty for . . . and recovery": ibid.

p. 250: killing nearly two hundred thousand civilians: "The Atomic Bombings of Hiroshima and Nagasaki," AtomicArchive.com, http://www.atomicarchive.com/Docs/MED/med_chp10.shtml.

p. 251: "no parades, no ceremonies" and "slipped away from the army and vanished from history": Gerard, p. 320.

p. 251: "like good soldiers, . . . what they did": ibid., p. 322.

BIBLIOGRAPHY

Ambrose, Stephen E. *D-Day, June 6, 1944: The Climactic Battle of World War II*. New York: Simon & Schuster, 1994.

Arnett, John. "The Ghost Army Days of Walter Wendell Arnett." Crescent Hill Baptist Church website, November 11, 2012. http://www.chbclky .org/arnettforest/wendell-ghostarmydays.htm.

Baker, Bob. "He Fought a War Armed with an Air Compressor: Secret WWII Unit Misled the Germans with Inflatable Tanks." *Los Angeles Times,* November 11, 1986. http://articles.latimes.com/1986-11-11/local /me-24864_1_air-compressor.

Ball, Peter. "Bridge of Wars—The Story of the Bailey Bridge." The Heritage Portal, November 22, 2016. http://www.theheritageportal.co.za /article/bridge-wars-story-bailey-bridge.

Barratt, John. "The Convoy System—Origins." MilitaryHistoryOnline.com. http://www.militaryhistoryonline.com/wwii/atlantic/convoy.aspx.

Battaglia, Andy. "How Fake Sound Recordings Helped Win World War II." Red Bull Music Academy Daily, Red Bull Music Academy, August 14, 2013. http://daily.redbullmusicacademy.com/2013/08/ghost-army -feature.

"Battle of the Bulge." History.net. http://www.historynet.com/battle-of -the-bulge.

Beevor, Antony. *Ardennes 1944: The Battle of the Bulge.* New York: Viking/ Penguin, 2015.

Beyer, Rick. "Freddy Fox Goes to War." *Princeton Alumni Weekly,* March 21, 2012. https://paw.princeton.edu/article/freddy-fox-goes-war.

Beyer, Rick, and Elizabeth Sayles. *Artists of Deception: The Ghost Army of World War II*. Plate of Peas Productions, 2011.

———. *The Ghost Army of World War II: How One Top-Secret Unit Deceived the Enemy with Inflatable Tanks, Sound Effects, and Other Audacious Fakery.* New York: Princeton Architectural Press, 2015.

Bradley, Omar N., and Clay Blair. *A General's Life.* New York: Simon & Schuster, 1983.

Breuer, William B. *Hoodwinking Hitler: The Normandy Deception.* Westport, CT: Praeger, 1993.

"Capturing the Bridge at Remagen, 1945." EyeWitness to History, 2008. http://www.eyewitnesstohistory.com/remagen.htm.

Chen, C. Peter. "Battle of the Bulge." World War II Database. http://ww2db .com/battle_spec.php?battle_id=42.

———. "Battle of the Scheldt Estuary." World War II Database. http:// ww2db.com/battle_spec.php?battle_id=116.

———. "Crossing the Rhine." World War II Database. http://ww2db.com /battle_spec.php?battle_id=134.

Cole, Hugh M. "The Ardennes: Battle of the Bulge." Washington, DC: Office of the Chief of Military History, Department of the Army, 1965. U.S. Army Center of Military History website. http://www.history.army .mil/books/wwii/7-8/7-8_CONT.HTM#toc.

Colley, David P. "On the Road to Victory: The Red Ball Express." HistoryNet.com. http://www.historynet.com/red-ball-express.

———. *The Road to Victory: The Untold Story of World War II's Red Ball Express.* Washington, DC: Brassey's, 2000.

Crowdy, Terry. *Deceiving Hitler: Double Cross and Deception in World War II.* New York: Osprey, 2008.

Cruickshank, Charles. *Deception in World War II.* New York: Oxford University Press, 1979.

Dunnigan, James F., and Albert A. Nofi. *Victory and Deceit: Dirty Tricks at War.* New York: Morrow, 1995.

Dwight David Eisenhower: The Centennial. Washington, DC: U.S. Army Center of Military History, 1990. U.S. Army Center of Military History website. http://www.history.army.mil/brochures/Ike/ike.htm.

Dwyer, John B. *Seaborne Deception: The History of U.S. Navy Beach Jumpers.* New York: Praeger, 1992.

Eisenhower, Dwight D. *Crusade in Europe.* New York: Doubleday, 1948.

Fairbanks, Douglas, Jr. *A Hell of a War.* New York: St. Martin's, 1993.

———. *The Salad Days.* New York: Doubleday, 1988.

"Fortress Metz: The 3rd Army's Toughest Battle." *MilitaryHistoryBlogspot,* August 26, 2014. https://militaryhistoryblogspot.wordpress. com/2014/08/26/fortress-metz-the-3rd-armys-toughest-battle/.

Fox, Capt. Frederic. "Official History of the 23rd Headquarters Special

Troops." Unpublished unit history. Box 23270, RG 407, National Archives at College Park, College Park, MD.

———. "The Deception Team: War and Football Are Getting Tougher." Unpublished manuscript. Dwight D. Eisenhower Library, Abilene, KS.

Fussell, Paul. *Wartime: Understanding and Behavior in the Second World War.* New York: Oxford University Press, 1989.

Gawne, Jonathan. *Ghosts of the ETO: American Tactical Deception Units in the European Theatre, 1944–1945.* Havertown, PA: Casemate, 2002.

Gerard, Philip. *Secret Soldiers: The Story of World War II's Heroic Army of Deception.* New York: Dutton, 2002.

Goodman, Steve. *Sonic Warfare: Sound, Affect, and the Ecology of Fear.* Cambridge, MA: MIT Press, 2009.

Gwatkin-Williams, Capt. R. S. "World War 2: Convoy Was the Key to Defeat of U-Boats Last Time." *Telegraph,* September 14, 2009. http://www.telegraph.co.uk/history/world-war-two/6188120/World-War-2-Convoy-was-the-key-to-defeat-of-U-boats-last-time.html.

"Half-Track Personnel Carrier M3 Multi-Purpose Armored Personal Carrier." Military Factory website, last updated March 16, 2017, http://www.militaryfactory.com/armor/detail.asp?armor_id=71.

Harrington, John Walker. "How Self-Taught Lumberjack Invented the World's First Endless-Tread Logging Tractor." *Popular Science,* January 1923, p. 46.

Heckman, Kristin E., Frank J. Stech, Roshan K. Thomas, Ben Schmoker, and Alexander W. Tsow. *Cyber Denial, Deception and Counter Deception.* New York: Springer, 2015.

Hemingway, Ernest. *Hemingway on War.* New York: Scribner, 2003.

Hickman, Kennedy. "World War II: Operation Market-Garden." ThoughtCo., updated January 6, 2017. https://www.thoughtco.com/world-war-ii-operation-market-garden-2361452.

"The History of the Corps of Engineers." 150th Combat Engineer Battalion of WWII website. http://www.150th.com/history/en_hist.htm.

Hollway, Don. "Otto Skorzeny and Operation Greif." Warfare History Network, January 19, 2016. http://warfarehistorynetwork.com/daily/wwii/otto-skorzeny-and-operation-grief/.

Holt, Thaddeus. *The Deceivers: Allied Military Deception in the Second World War.* New York: Scribner, 2004.

Ingersoll, Ralph. *Top Secret.* New York: Harcourt, Brace, 1946.

Jentz, Brianna M. "Blarney in WWII: An Overview of the 23rd Special Headquarters' Deceptive Ways." Research paper, University of Wisconsin-Platteville, 2012. https://www.uwplatt.edu/files/urce /Jentz.pdf.

Kneece, Jack. *Ghost Army of World War II.* Gretna, LA: Pelican, 2001.

Korell, Kirsten. "Germans in Argentina: Two Testimonies from Comodoro Rivadavia." Patagonia Mosaic 2001: Migration, Work, and Community in Comodoro Rivadavis and Its Oil Company Towns, Dickinson College. http://deila.dickinson.edu/patagonia/newsite/mosaic01pat /projectsGermansKorell.html#German%20Immigration%20in%20 Argentina.

Latimer, Jon. *Deception in War: The Art of the Bluff, the Value of Deceit, and the Most Thrilling Episodes of Cunning in Military History, from the Trojan Horse to the Gulf War.* Woodstock, NY: Overlook, 2001.

Lee, Bill. "The Liberty Ships of World War II: Their Union County and Other Carolina Connections." J. A. Jones, Inc., website. http://www.jajones .com/pdf/Liberty_Ships_of_WWII.pdf.

Levine, Joshua. *Operation Fortitude: The Story of the Spies and the Spy Operation that Saved D-Day.* Guilford, CT: Lyons, 2012.

"Liberty Ships Built by the United States Maritime Commission in World War II." American Merchant Marine at War website. http://www.usmm .org/libertyships.html.

Lippman, David. "Operation Plunder: Crossing the Rhine." Warfare History Network, September 15, 2016. http://warfarehistorynetwork.com /daily/wwii/operation-plunder-crossing-the-rhine/.

Loewy, Tom. "Vet Shares Stores of Ghost Army." *Galesburg Register-Mail,* May 25, 2014. http://www.galesburg.com/article/20140525/NEWS /140529801?template=printart.

———. *The Last Offensive.* The United States Army in World War II: The European Theater of Operations. Washington, D.C.: United States Army Center of Military History, 1972. Reprinted 1993. United States Army Center of Military History website. www.history.army.mil/html /books/007/7-9-1/CMH_Pub_7-9-1.pdf.

Macintyre, Ben. *Operation Mincemeat: How a Dead Man and a Bizarre Plan Fooled the Nazis and Assured an Allied Victory.* New York: Harmony, 2010.

Merryman, Richard. "A Painter of Angels Became the Father of

Camouflage." Smithsonian, April 1999. http://www.smithsonianmag
.com/arts-culture/a-painter-of-angels-became-the-father-of-
camouflage-67218866/.

Montagu, Ewen. *The Man Who Never Was.* Philadelphia: Lippincott, 1954.

Moore, Sam. "Lombard's Log Hauler: The First Crawler Tractor." *Farm
Collector,* November 2001.

Murray, Kelly. "The Planning of 'Operation Overlord." In "The Longest
Day." Research paper, Mount Holyoke College, 2008. https://
www.mtholyoke.edu/~kmmurray/The%20Longest%20Day
/planning%20operation%20overlord.html.

"A 'Neutral' Power? American Involvement in WW2 Before Pearl Harbor."
Military History Now website. http://militaryhistorynow.com/2013
/01/09/the-war-before-the-war-americas-pre-pearl-harbor-
involvement-in-ww2/.

Paltrow, Gwyneth. "Ellsworth Kelly." *Interview,* September 24, 2011.
http://www.interviewmagazine.com/art/ellsworth-kelly/#_.

Park, Edwards. "A Phantom Division Played a Vital Role in Germany's
Defeat." *Smithsonian,* April 1985: 138–147.

Patton, George S., Jr. *War As I Knew It.* Boston: Houghton Mifflin, 1947.

Persico, Joseph E. *Piercing the Reich: The Penetration of Nazi Germany by
American Secret Agents During World War II.* New York: Viking, 1979.

Rankin, Nicholas. *Churchill's Wizards: The British Genius for Deception,
1914–1945.* London: Faber & Faber, 2009.

Riddle, Perry C. "Reflections: 'That's When We Really Knew That We Were
Going to Be Decoys, Sitting Ducks.'" *Los Angeles Times,* June 10, 1986.
http://articles.latimes.com/1986-06-10/local/me-9866_1_tanks.

Rodgers, Russ. "Breakout and Exploitation: Normandy July–August 1944."
Research paper, American Military University, September 2004.
https://docslide.com.br/documents/breakout-and-exploitation
-normandy-july-august-1944.html.

Ruppenthal, Roland G. *Logistical Support of the Armies.* 2 vols. The United
States Army in World War II: The European Theater of Operations.
Washington, D.C.: Center of Military History, 1953. Reprinted 1995.

Sanders, Gold V. "Push-Over Bridges Built Like Magic from Interlocking
Parts." *Popular Science,* October 1944: 94.

"Ships Hit By U-Boats in WWII: Ship Losses by Month." Uboat.net. http://
uboat.net/allies/merchants/losses_year.html.

Stokesbury, James L. *A Short History of World War II.* New York: Harper Perennial, 2001.

"Timeline of the Normandy Breakout (July 1944)." Second World War History website. http://www.secondworldwarhistory.com/normandy-breakout.asp.

"US Entry and Alliance." In "History of WW2." History Channel UK website. http://www.history.co.uk/topics/history-of-ww2/us-entry-and-alliance.

Wilson, E. Gordon, Jr. *Normandy to Germany with the Ghost Army, 1944–1945.* Self-published, 1997.

IMAGE CREDITS

(Washington, DC: Office of the Chief of Military History, Department of the Army, 1956).

p. 66: Photograph reprinted courtesy of Project Liberty Ship, Inc., SS *John W. Brown*

p. 67: Courtesy of the Harry S. Truman Library

p. 68: Courtesy of the Leamington Courier Series; source: Warwickshire County Record Office

pp. 72 (both images), 81, 82, and 86: Courtesy of the National Archives

p. 88: Copyright © by the Imperial War Museum

p. 89: Courtesy of the Library of Congress, Prints and Photographs Division

p. 90: Courtesy of the National Archives, Department of Defense, Department of the Army. Office of the Deputy Chief of Staff for Operations. U.S. Army Audiovisual Center

p. 93: Photograph courtesy of Donald Fox

p. 94: Courtesy of the Library of Congress, Prints and Photographs Division

p. 95: Photograph copyright © by Roger-Viollet/Getty Images. Reprinted with permission.

p. 97: Barcroft/Barcroft Media/Getty Images. Reprinted with permission.

p. 120: Courtesy of the National Archives

p. 126: Courtesy of the National Archives, Department of Defense, Department of the Army, Office of the Deputy Chief of Staff for Operations, U.S. Army Audiovisual Center

p. 132: Courtesy of the National Archives

p. 147: Courtesy of the National Archives/U.S. Army Signal Corps

p. 152: Courtesy of the National Archives

p. 155: Photograph 12/Universal Images/Getty Images. Reprinted with permission.

p. 161: Image reprinted with permission of the Estate of Arthur Singer

p. 163: Courtesy of the U.S. Army Signal Corps

p. 171: Copyright © by Hampshire County Council. Provided by the Hampshire Cultural Trust.

p. 174: Courtesy of the National Archives

p. 180: Courtesy of the U.S. Army Quartermaster Museum

p. 186: Courtesy of the Library of Congress, Prints and Photographs Division

p. 187: Photograph copyright © by John Florea/LIFE Picture Collection /Getty Images. Reprinted with permission.

p. 191: Painting by Robert N. Blair. Courtesy of the U.S. Army Center of Military History.

p. 193: Courtesy of the U.S. Army Center of Military History

p. 204: Copyright © by Roger-Viollet/Getty Images. Reprinted with permission.

pp. 206–207: Photograph copyright © by Barcroft/Barcroft Media/Getty Images Reprinted with permission.

p. 210: Courtesy of the National Archives

p. 214: Photograph courtesy of Claude Truong-Ngoc

p. 222: Courtesy of the National Archives/U.S. Army Signal Corps

p. 231: Courtesy of the Imperial War Museum

p. 234: Courtesy of the National Archives, Office for Emergency Management, Office of War Information, Overseas Operations Branch. New York. News and Features Bureau.

p. 237: Courtesy of the U.S. Army

p. 243: Courtesy of the Imperial War Museum

p. 244: Facsimile of original document from the National Archives

p. 251: Courtesy of the National Archives, WWII Operations Report, Special Troops

INDEX

Note: Page numbers in italics indicate images and/or caption text.

ACKNOWLEDGMENTS

Thank you to Brianna Jentz Kirschbaum, my crackerjack researcher and maker of spreadsheets, who kept track of matters that would have done me in.

Thank you to Lynn Smith, who graciously gave me access to her father's memoir of his time with the Twenty-Third.